Pam led Bill into the bedroom she shared with Gregg and put a Van Halen CD on the player. Then she excused herself and disappeared into the bathroom.

When she came out five minutes later she was wearing a turquoise negligee she had bought especially for the occasion. Then she punched a few buttons on the CD player and walked to the center of the room.

When the steady beat of Pam's favorite selection from the album began reverberating off the bedroom walls, she started taking off the negligee. With increasing frenzy she undid the buttons on it while Bill sat there goggle-eyed. When the song ended, the negligee ended up in a pile on the floor. So did Pam and Bill.

That was Bill's sexual initiation. The next morning, as Pam was driving them both to school, he got the second half of the lesson, an initiation into the world of cynicism.

"Last night was great," Pam said, "but we can't keep on like that."

"Why not?" he wanted to know.

"Because of Gregg. If you want to keep seeing me, you'll have to get rid of my husband."

St. Martin's Paperbacks
by Ken Englade

CELLAR OF HORROR

BEYOND REASON

MURDER IN BOSTON

DEADLY LESSONS

DEADLY LESSONS

KEN ENGLADE

SMP

ST. MARTIN'S PAPERBACKS

DEADLY LESSONS

Copyright © 1991 by Ken Englade.

Cover photographs courtesy AP/Wide World Photos.

ISBN: 0-312-92761-4

Printed in the United States of America

St. Martin's Paperbacks edition/July 1991

10 9 8 7 6 5 4 3

For Don and Robin

Acknowledgments

My thanks to Tom Bartlett, to Tom Bonner and WMUR-TV, and, especially, to my editors, Maureen O'Neal and Charles Spicer, for their patience and unflagging enthusiasm.

1

Tuesday, May 1, 1990
Derry, New Hampshire
8:30 P.M.

THEY WAITED IN THE DARK, two gangly teenagers not yet old enough to attend an R-rated
movie. One was called Pete and the other Bill.

As the minutes ticked away, their agitation
grew. Nervously they glanced at each other.

"Where the hell is he?" Pete whispered.

"I don't know," Bill muttered, "but I wish to
hell he'd hurry up."

He did a quick little jig, rearranging the unfa-
miliar and uncomfortable object he had stuck in
his waistband: a snub-nosed revolver that
another friend, J.R., had sneaked out of his
father's gun collection.

"Tell me again how we're going to handle
this," demanded Pete.

"You're going to get behind the door and I'm
going to get on the stairs where he can't see me.
Then when he opens the door you're going to
pull him inside and we'll both jump him. Then
you're going to cut his throat."

"Right," Pete replied, changing his grip on the

long-handled knife he had picked up as they'd walked through the kitchen a few minutes earlier.

The only light in the room was what filtered through a small window that opened onto the parking lot. In the weak glow the two could have passed for brothers, which is what they proclaimed themselves to be anyway, in spirit if not by blood. They were dressed identically in sweats and tattered sneakers, and each wore latex gloves over fingers wrapped in scotch tape. Despite their ninjalike outfits, they had a fresh-scrubbed, still innocent look, a look that most definitely contradicted their reason for being in unit 4E on Misty Morning Drive.

Bill stood impatiently in the kitchen. Chewing his lip, he watched the window as intently as if it were a television tuned to his favorite channel, MTV. But there wasn't any picture and there wasn't any sound except the thudding of his heart and the muffled whimper of a dog, a plaintive whine he happily noted was growing less insistent by the minute.

Pete sat at the dining table, nervously fingering the long-bladed knife, whose handle he had wrapped with a paper towel in a spasm of paranoia over the possibility of leaving fingerprints.

They exchanged very few words because there was no need for conversation. They had been best friends since the eighth grade, and over the years they had traded every imaginable confidence. As a result, they were as attuned to each other's thoughts as an old married couple. At that time, to discuss *anything* except their reason for being there would have been inane. So they waited in silence.

This was Bill's third attempt to confront and kill Gregory Smart. He had botched the other two plans, and if he screwed up this one, he and Pame would be finished. She had made that very clear: If you don't do it this time, you'll never see me again. It was a hell of a position to be in, especially for a sixteen-year-old who for the first time in his short life was getting steady and abundant sex. Not only that, but the source of his bliss was an older woman, a slim, beautiful twenty-two-year-old who, until two and a half months ago, had seemed totally unapproachable.

"How long do you think we're going to have to wait?" Pete asked, trying to sound casual.

"As long as we have to," Bill answered. "You have everything?"

Pete pointed to the dark shape on the floor by the kitchen door, a black pillowcase filled with CDs and costume jewelry.

"All ready to go. All we need is Gregg."

Seemingly in response to his statement, a pair of powerful headlights lit up the window. An engine rumbled throatily.

"That's him!" Bill said excitedly. "That's his truck."

As if on strings, the two youths hustled to get into their agreed-upon positions. But in the excitement they got their places reversed: Bill jumped behind the door, and Pete hid on the stairs. The bright light that had briefly illuminated the room was suddenly extinguished, along with the noise of the engine. Seconds later they heard a vehicle door open, then slam shut. That in turn was followed by the sound of footsteps. They heard a key go into the lock, and they stood as if frozen as the door swung open.

Gregg Smart, a twenty-four-year-old neophyte insurance salesman, five feet ten and 170 hard pounds toned by skiing, fishing, and hiking through the New England forests, stood on the threshold.

"Halen," he called, signaling the dog that he was home.

When the puppy failed to appear, a look of concern started across his brow. But before he could move, Bill reached out and dragged him inside.

Gregg screamed and tried to run, heading for the door. But Bill was too quick. Clamping a hand on Gregg's shoulder, he threw him against the foyer wall and started pounding him with his fists, hitting him wherever he could.

As Gregg raised his arms to protect his face, Pete stepped forward, grabbing a handful of Gregg's hair in his left hand. With a quick push, he bounced Gregg's head against the wall—hard —and the resistance evaporated. Still holding his hair, Pete forced Gregg to his knees.

Gregg began to whimper loudly.

"Shut up!" Pete commanded. "Just shut up!"

At the same time, he raised his free right hand, the one in which he held the knife. Moving the blade to be sure that Gregg could see it, Pete stuck the tip under Gregg's chin, indicating that it would be in Gregg's best interest to remain as quiet as possible.

"Have you hurt Halen?" Gregg asked, his eyes rolling in fear.

"Don't worry about the dog," Bill growled, astounded that anyone could think about an animal at a time like this. "He's okay."

"Please don't hurt him," Gregg pleaded. "I'll give you whatever you want."

"Give me your wallet," Pete ordered.

Digging it out of his pocket, he handed it to Pete, who passed it to Bill. He removed the bills and threw it on the floor.

"Is that all?" Pete asked. "Give me your chain."

"I don't have a chain," Gregg stuttered. "Take whatever you want. Just don't kill me. Please don't kill me."

When Gregg handed over his billfold, Pete had seen the flash of gold on his finger. "Give me your ring," he demanded.

Gregg stared at him in disbelief. "No!" he said emphatically. "I can't do that."

Taken aback, Pete was not sure how to respond. "What do you mean, 'no'?" he asked, shocked by the unexpected resistance.

"My wife would kill me," Gregg added. "It's my wedding ring."

That simple statement, extraordinary under the circumstances, visibly unnerved Pete. The hand that was holding the knife wavered, and he looked confused. In that instant fear rippled through his body like an electric shock, and his resolve to slice Gregg's jugular disappeared abruptly.

Bill, sensing his friend's sudden change in attitude, motioned to catch Pete's eye. Without a word he pointed to his waist, where the pistol was tucked into the sweatpants. The message was clear. Pete nodded.

Drawing the gun, Bill cocked the hammer and lowered it with a shaking hand until the barrel was only two inches from the back of Gregg's head at a point just to the rear of his left ear. He was behind Gregg and out of his line of sight.

"God forgive me," Bill said softly, squeezing the trigger. When he did, a .38-caliber hollow-point slug, a projectile designed to fragment on impact and cause the maximum amount of destruction possible, crashed into Gregg's brain. He died without ever hearing the shot that killed him.

"Jesus," gulped Pete, realizing he was holding the head of a dead man. "Let's get out of here."

Recovering quickly, they turned on their heels and raced for the back door. Bill went out first, followed by Pete. As he ran through the door, Pete reached up and, without breaking stride, swept up the pillowcase filled with loot. He was two steps behind his friend as they dashed across an empty lot that separated the cluster of condominiums from the back of a small mall, Hood Plaza, less than a football field away. As they ran, Pete discarded the knife and Bill began peeling off his gloves. They stopped momentarily when they got to a dumpster in the rear of a doctor's office. Bill threw his gloves at the yawning opening. One went inside and the other fell to the ground. Later, it would be recovered by a state policeman, who, thinking it was part of the regular detritus from the medical facility, would throw it away.

A few seconds later they reached a road that ran around the rear of the mall. As they did, a Chevrolet Impala pulled up.

Bill reached the car first. He clambered inside, followed closely by Pete, who slammed the door and yelled at the driver, J.R.: "Go! Go! Go!"

"Why?"

"We killed somebody, we killed somebody."

J.R. glanced at his friend, who was deathly pale. I've got to calm him down, J.R. thought. I've got to get him to laugh. "Hey," he said, "let's sing."

As J.R. swung out of Derry onto State Route 102, which would connect with Highway 101 and take them eastward, back to their homes in Seabrook, he broke into an off-key rendition of "Shoo Fly Pie."

The selection was so ludicrous, Bill could not

help grinning. Soon he began to giggle. God, he thought, it's great to have friends.

A few doors down from the Smart condominium, Fred Lombardi was hosting a celebration for his youngest son. At around ten P.M., just about the time the carload of singing teenagers was pulling into Seabrook, Lombardi was leading his guests into "Happy Birthday" when the sing-along was interrupted by a woman's piercing scream.

What the hell is that? Lombardi wondered. A woman screaming in the middle of the night in their small condominium complex was unprecedented. The small cluster of wooden town houses, less than a mile from the town's police headquarters, was occupied mostly by young couples who worked hard all day, retired and rose early, especially on weeknights, and generally kept pretty much to themselves. Outside of an occasional overloud stereo or the screech of a vehicle taking off too quickly, loud noises were virtually nonexistent.

Dashing outside, Lombardi almost collided with Pamela Smart, who was running away from the condo she and her husband, Gregg, had occupied for almost a year.

"What is it?" Lombardi asked anxiously. "What's the matter? What's happened?"

"It's my husband," she answered. "He's been killed! He's dead!"

Not sure she was acting rationally, Lombardi

started toward the Smart residence. "I'll see," he said. "Maybe it isn't as bad as you think."

"No!" Pam yelled, bringing him up short. "Don't go in there. It wouldn't do any good. He's dead. I just know it."

Lombardi looked at the unit she had just exited; it was as dark as the inside of a closet. Unwillingly, a thought flashed into his head. How does she know he's dead? he wondered. She didn't even turn the light on.

"I think I ought to check first," Lombardi told her, moving toward the door. "Maybe I can help."

"Please," Pam begged. "Don't go in there. Just call the police." Then she asked cryptically, "Why do they keep doing this?"

Lombardi stared. "What did you say?" he asked.

"Why do they keep doing this?" she repeated.

Lombardi shrugged. She must be in shock, he thought. His son, who had been watching the exchange, sprinted to the telephone and dialed 911.

2

DERRY IS NOT A LARGE TOWN, only thirty-two thousand residents, and a lot of the people know each other. In Derry you don't have to be a politician to be well known; an industrious insurance salesman can get around to lots of households. On that balmy May Day evening, while one of Gregg's neighbors was calling the police, another was dialing William and Judith Smart, Gregg's parents. "You'd better come over here," he told Gregg's father, "I think Gregg is sick or something."

Since they lived only a block away, the Smarts almost beat the police there. Almost, but not quite. When William and Judith and another son, Dean, arrived, there already was a police guard at Pam and Gregg's door. The officer, acting under orders, refused to let them in or tell them what had happened.

"For God's sake," pleaded Dean, a thin, bespectacled, dark-haired man who looked like a junior faculty member from a small college, "will somebody tell us what's wrong with Gregg?"

When they got the news fifteen minutes later, they were devastated. All of them, apparently, but Pam, who as far as anyone could determine never shed a tear.

After Gregg's body was taken away, William, Judith, and Pam returned to the elder Smart's home since the condo was still under police seal.

"Good God," moaned William, "how could this have happened?" Sitting at the kitchen table, bolstered by a pot of strong, fresh coffee, he unconsciously rubbed his white mustache. With the facial hair, a ruddy complexion, and deep crow's-feet that made him look as if he had spent uncounted hours squinting into the sun, William more closely resembled a character out of a western than the supersalesman of insurance that he was.

His wife, Judith, was on the verge of falling to pieces. A tall, slim woman with blond hair cut fashionably short, she seemed inconsolable. Before twenty-four hours passed, William would have to take her to the hospital and have her sedated.

The only totally calm one in the group was Pam. Crisp and cool in her dress-for-success business suit, she sipped calmly from her cup. "I wish someone would tell me if Halen is all right," she said, apropos of nothing.

Judith's mouth fell open. She could not believe that her daughter-in-law was worrying about her pet while her husband was stretched out in a morgue, a victim of murder. She was on the verge of saying something, but then she thought better of it. Pam is just being Pam, she told herself, saying whatever comes into her head to prevent revealing what she was *really* feeling. In the three years she had known Pam, Judith had come to accept her as an eccentric but apparently well-meaning person, to realize that her son's wife was a very private individual who seldom displayed emotion. She definitely had strange ways, Judith had decided, such as her rigid insistence on storing her clothes in color-coordinated groupings and her habit of folding her soiled clothing before stacking the pile neatly in one of the two hampers she kept in her closet, one for white, one for dark. Or the fact that Pam ran her entire life on a tight schedule and tended to become unduly upset if an unforeseen occurrence caused her plan to deviate from the expected. But everyone was entitled to a few quirks, Judith reasoned, and Pam seemed to have been good for Gregg even if she was wound a little too tightly.

William figured Pam was in shock and didn't know what she was saying. "Tell us what you know," he prodded.

"I don't know anything," Pam said without emotion. "I had to go to a school board meeting, and when I got home I found Gregg dead on the floor."

Judith blew her nose. "I can't believe it," she

said. "I can't believe he's dead. He was so full of life; he was so happy about the way things were going. You were going to celebrate your first anniversary next week—a week from yesterday—and he had big plans for that."

Gregg had confided in his parents that he planned a party to celebrate the occasion and that later he and Pam planned to fly to Florida so she could log some beach time. "If there's anything Pam really loves," Gregg had told his parents once, "it's lying on the beach. She's a real sun bunny."

William shook his head. It just didn't make sense. Murders were rare in Derry; Gregg's was the first of 1990. As it turned out, it would be the *only* one in the town that year, but the Smarts had no way of knowing that at the time.

"Why do you think he was killed?" he asked Pam, trying desperately to get a focus on the tragedy that had enveloped the family.

"Burglars," Pam said evenly. "They were robbing the place, and Gregg came home and surprised them. So they killed him."

Later, William would ask himself how Pam knew that. She had barely set foot in the door; in fact, she had not even turned on the light before she'd run screaming into the parking lot. How could she possibly have known that the condo had been ransacked? But at the time her statements rang no warning bells.

If he had been thinking clearly, William also might have asked himself why a burglar had picked the early evening to do a job, a time when people were likely to be stirring about and a stranger's presence would be noticed immediately, particularly in a small housing complex like Pam and Gregg's, where most of the residents were working couples who were in their houses at dinnertime. Burglaries also were relatively rare in Derry, especially in the section where the young couple lived, and if one wanted to strike there, it seemed best to hit during the day when everyone was gone rather than early in the evening.

The police later would ask themselves these same questions and many more, some of which never would have occurred to William and Judith, such as what could Gregg possibly have done to force a burglar, provided a thief was the real culprit, to kill? Burglars, they knew, usually did not go armed. And crime statistics showed burglars committed homicides only under the most drastic of circumstances. Even when they did commit murder, it was seldom an execution-style killing such as that committed upon Gregg Smart.

From the very beginning, Derry Police Chief Edward Garone and his investigators suspected they were seeing something that someone wanted them to see, not something that really was. But it would take days, eventually weeks, for these theories to be articulated sufficiently to form a viable pattern of suspicion. In the meantime, both investigators and family members had to accept the facts for what they appeared to be: that a young man just beginning to hit his stride in life had been brutally murdered by a person or persons unknown, for a reason or reasons that were equally mysterious.

Not everyone in the family, however, was willing to accept the status quo. Dean Smart, the eldest of William and Judith's three sons, asked himself many of the same questions that his parents and the police were asking. The difference was, he came to an earlier and more radical conclusion. Less than twenty-four hours after Gregg's murder, he was hashing over the situation with his fiancée, and the discussion kept coming back to one point: The story as outlined by Pam did not hang together.

"There's something fishy here," Dean said, "I just can't put my finger on it. I hope I'm wrong, but I can't help feeling that Pam had something to do with it."

But that intuition was not something he was ready to express to anyone else, not for a long time to come. Publicly he would continue to defend Pam for weeks after the murder.

However, at the Smarts' house that first night, grief had not yet given way to skepticism. William, Judith—and ostensibly Pam—were each trying to come to terms with the tragedy according to the dictates of their individual personalities. William brooded. Judith sobbed. And Pam seemed to be wandering on another planet.

"I *wish* they would tell me about my dog," she said. "I just want to know if he's all right."

The initial feelings of unease the Smarts experienced were heightened a few days later when Gregg's body was being prepared for burial. William and Judith arranged for *two* ceremonies, one in Londonderry, where Gregg had grown up, and one in Derry, where he was living when he was killed. The service in Derry's St. Thomas Aquinas Church, on May 4, drew almost four hundred mourners.

Before the funeral there was a wake, which also drew a number of friends and acquaintances. Among them were two teenagers: Bill and J.R., who came all the way from Seabrook, a forty-five-minute drive away.

But what people noticed at the wake was not the appearance of Bill and J.R., whom no one except Pam recognized anyway, but the behavior of Pam Smart. It was at that service that Pam acted peculiarly enough to attract the attention of those other than the immediate family. While Gregg's body lay in an open casket in a viewing room at the Peabody Funeral Home in Londonderry, Pam waited in an adjoining room. As friends and relatives filed in to pay their final respects, Pam steadfastly remained outside, seemingly distancing herself from the Smarts. When it was suggested that she go into the room where Gregg's body lay in state to say her last good-bye, she refused to enter until a funeral home employee went in first and closed the casket. She was adamant about not having to look upon Gregg's remains.

This aberration was noted by several people, but it went unremarked upon until many days later, when the episodes that occurred in the first hours after Gregg's death were put into a different perspective. Long before the summer was over, the circumstances surrounding Gregg's murder would take on a whole new light.

3

ALMOST FROM THE TIME she discovered her husband's body, Pam's behavior was unusual. But it would still be many days before those who lived through those times began comparing notes and putting bits and pieces together. Viewed in retrospect, it is hard to understand why no one said anything sooner. However, part of the answer to that may lie in the attitude that prevails throughout New Hampshire, a state that prides itself upon individualism and personal freedom.

The state's motto, reproduced among other places on license plates and the masthead of the state's most influential newspaper, the Manchester *Union Leader*, is "Live free or die," a quote from General John Stark, a Londonderry soldier who fought in the Revolutionary War battles of Bunker Hill and Bennington and went on to command the Continental Army's Northern Department. The motto would later have a startlingly ironic meaning for Pam, considering her ultimate fate. But in New Hampshire, an individual's right to be different is highly prized, even when a murder has been committed. It would be a long time before Judith Smart would mention to anyone outside the family that she thought it was extremely strange how Pam remained dry-eyed the night of Gregg's death, when everyone else was dissolving in grief; that Pam seemed more worried about her dog than about her dead husband. It would be months before Judith would relate how Pam refused to view her husband's body or how her daughter-in-law, two days after her husband was killed, returned his belongings to his parents jammed inside black plastic garbage bags. She would be even more reluctant to reveal how shocked she had been when, soon after Gregg's murder, she visited Pam at her new condo and was unable to find a single picture of Gregg on display anywhere in the dwelling.

At the time, Judith and William thought they were the only ones noticing these things, that their view of what was occurring was clouded by grief and they were not seeing life through an objective lens. What they did *not* know was that others also were noting Pam's strange behavior and, although hesitant to mention it to anyone else, filed the incidents away to be drawn out later after the situation turned upside down.

Take the issue of news coverage, for example. Although the area newspapers reported the crime, the coverage was restrained by the fact that the Derry police had put a tight lid on information, refusing to say much more than that a man named Gregory Smart had indeed been shot and killed in his condominium.

A good example was the story that appeared in the Nashua *Telegraph* on May 3, two days after the murder, under the headline DERRY FAMILY SHATTERED BY MURDER. The pertinent paragraph read: "Derry Police Capt. Loring Jackson said the crime probably wasn't a random attack or the result of a botched burglary. He would not comment on any possible motives or suspects."

Jackson, it was made clear later, was not playing games with the media; he was simply protecting his investigation. Police, although not sure exactly what to make of the crime, were fairly certain that it was not as clear-cut as it appeared. So until they could resolve the paramount issues, they decided to say nothing at all.

This policy, needless to say, did not sit well with Pam. Within thirty-six hours of her husband's murder, even before he was buried, she began telephoning area news agencies, volunteering to be interviewed about his death or dispersing tips about the crime.

Tami Plyler, a correspondent for the *Union Leader*, interviewed Pam on May 9, eight days after Gregg's murder. Greeting the newswoman clad casually in jeans, Pam curled up on a sofa in her mother's house in Canobie Lake and discoursed freely about the situation.

"I think about what our dreams were and

[how] those things will never happen," Plyler quoted her as saying. "But I'm still alive and I still have dreams. I will try to go forward and do those things."

Writing about the interview later, Plyler revealed how she had been impressed with Pam's apparent strength and how determined she seemed to be to continue with her life in spite of the tragedy. "She spoke at length," Plyler wrote, "of her plan to set up a fund in her husband's name for a media course" she wanted to teach. "Every kid who comes through that course," Pam said, "I have confidence I will touch their lives and Gregg will also."

Even before the Plyler interview, Pam had been quoted in newspapers and on TV as asking anyone who might have knowledge of the crime to come forward and share their knowledge with investigators. In her chat with the reporter, she carried this theme another step forward.

"People want me to try to explain why such a senseless thing could happen," Pam said. "People want me to try to explain why I can't explain this. They're searching their own minds for a reason, and I can't give them one. I'd love to have one to give them, but I don't know, and that's the hardest part."

She had gotten through the catastrophe, she said, by calling upon an inner reserve that she had never known she had. Other people, she added, had this inner strength as well, and many of them didn't realize it until they needed it.

Asked by Plyler if she had anything she would like to pass on to others who were then or one day might be facing the same demands, Pam said: "I'd tell them to try to set their minds at ease and not go over the questions they might have, and realize that life is just not always fair."

Nancy West, a reporter for the New Hampshire *Sunday News*, a special weekly edition of the *Union Leader*, also interviewed Pam after waving her over when she saw her driving down the street. Although West's interview came more than a month after Plyler's and there had been significant developments in the murder investigation by then, many of the ideas expressed by Pam were similar to the ones she had revealed to Plyler.

Her life with Gregg, she said, had been "picture perfect" and nothing she did in the future would be able to equal what she had shared with her husband. "I'd like to try to start my life over," she said, "because Gregg would want it that way."

"She didn't seem like a happy woman that day," West wrote later, despite her attempt at optimism. "Her actions were guarded and she seemed a little scared." But West confessed she could see nothing in Pam's talk or behavior that indicated she might have been involved in a serious crime.

* * *

In an interview with the Nashua *Telegraph*, Pam was asked how she managed to adjust so well. She replied: "I have faith that I'll be okay, and I'm a really strong person. I know that everything I do for the rest of my life—he'll always be a part of me. He's physically gone, but he's not gone from my heart."

She and Gregg, she said, were looking forward to their trip to Florida because they wanted to use the time to renew their relationship. "At this time last year we were getting all ready for our wedding, and we were really happy about that and our whole future together."

Overall, the reporters who interviewed her seemed to have come away from their contacts with Pam affected by her apparent sincerity. One reporter, however, had an entirely different feeling about his encounter with the young widow.

Bill Spencer, who specializes in crime coverage at Manchester's WMUR-TV, was contacted by Pam less than two days after Gregg's murder. At the time, Spencer had virtually nothing to report on the crime because of the police clampdown. But when Pam got him on the line, she complained bitterly that investigators were refusing to tell the public that Gregg had been killed during a burglary attempt and that he had been shot by intruders.

Spencer dutifully took notes as Pam spoke, but

when she finished he had a question, not about the crime, but about her strategy.

"Why did you call me?" he asked, wondering why he had been singled out as the recipient of such a hot tip.

That was simple, Pam said. "I'm fascinated by your murder stories, and I never dreamed that I'd be part of one of them."

Her response, more in the way she said it than in what she said, sent a chill down Spencer's spine. Later he would say it was at that moment that he began seriously to wonder about Pam's involvement.

4

THE ONE WHO SEEMED to take Gregg's death the hardest of all was his mother, Judith. Her and William's other sons, Dean and Rick, were loyal, loving children, but it was Gregg, who had perversely spelled his name with two *g*'s ever since he was a child, whom she had grown increasingly close to in recent months. He had been a late bloomer, but when his talent started to flower it made Judith as happy as she had ever been.

A free-spirited, fun-loving youth, Gregg had pretty much gone his own way most of his life. While many of his contemporaries were incredibly competitive in their teens, vying for spots on the athletic teams, on the honor roll, or in clubs, Gregg had gone through high school in neighboring Londonderry virtually invisibly. His picture was in the school annual for his senior year, 1983, but that was all. While other students had rows of small type under their portraits spelling out their achievements, Gregg had only his address under his picture, which was fine by him. A shy, quiet, rather reclusive youth, described by school officials as an average student, Gregg preferred fishing to football and hiking to history. But in one way he was not unlike his peers: he had an uncommon love for rock music. In emulation of the heavy-metal heroes of the day, Gregg strummed a guitar and let his hair grow to his shoulders.

Despite his apparent preference for anonymity, Gregg was an avid partygoer and an ardent admirer of the opposite sex. He also had a good sense of humor. Once, when a friend gave him a surprise party, he *really* surprised Gregg by inviting the five girls he was then dating. Instead of being embarrassed, Gregg thought it was a hoot. In fact, it was at a party—a New Year's Eve shindig, to be specific—at the end of 1986 that Gregg, then twenty-one, met a brash, petite, nineteen-year-old college student named Pamela Anne Wojas. Despite their obvious personality differences, differences that would become decidedly more pronounced in the future, the two hit it off immediately.

Pamela, who was called Pame (pronounced "Pammie") by her close friends, had her feet in two worlds: New Hampshire and Florida.

A native of Florida, Pam's father, John, her mother, Linda, and her older sister, Beth, lived in Miami until Pam was in the eighth grade. By then John Wojas, a commercial airline pilot, had become sufficiently worried about the increase in crime in south Florida to begin looking for someplace safe to move his family. He picked the community of Canobie Lake, near Windham in south central New Hampshire, a locale that could not have been more different from Miami. Furs and birches took the place of palms and pines. Instead of the Atlantic Ocean, there was a relatively small, almost circular freshwater lake whose banks were lined with two-story clapboard houses rather than the brick ranch-style homes common in Florida. Boundary dividers in New Hampshire tended to be constructed of rough boulders piled one atop another rather than the wire hurricane fences so common in Miami. McDonald's was supplanted by the Canobie Clam Box, and the pride of the community was a small waterside amusement park, complete with roller coaster and miniature riverboat, which plied the lake on summer evenings. Seeking solitude, tranquillity, and a decent place for his two daughters to grow up, John and Linda picked out a comfortable $225,000 home and moved in just about the time Pam was ready for high school.

One of the disadvantages of Canobie Lake was that it did not have its own secondary school. When its children reached the ninth grade, they were transported to Derry, a dozen or so miles to the north, to attend the Pinkerton Academy, a private school consisting of an eclectic collection of brick, ancient hand-cut stone, and modern frame buildings that wander over a hillside on the east side of town. Like Canobie Lake, several of the small communities around Derry had neither the resources nor the inclination to build their own high school, so the town governments contracted with Pinkerton to accept their students. It was a situation not unlike the one that exists in rural areas of other states where the teenagers attend a regional high school. Except in the case of Pinkerton the regional school was private rather than public.

The fact that Pinkerton students came from several nearby towns probably worked to Pam's advantage, in that she was regarded as less of an outsider than she might have been under other circumstances. As a result of that, as well as her wit and natural effusiveness, Pam adapted immediately to New Hampshire's close-knit community despite being a southern transplant.

In her freshman year at Pinkerton she was elected to the first of four terms she would serve as a homeroom representative and as a member of the Winter Carnival court. She also made the honor roll every year, a feat she achieved every year through college.

Beginning in her sophomore year, her 450 classmates elected her an officer as well as a member of the Student Council; she also began a three-year career as a basketball cheerleader. In her junior year she also became a cheerleader for the football team and dated the team's co-captain, a brawny youth nicknamed "Sausage." In her high school yearbook, one memorable picture shows her in her school letter sweater with her name, Pame, running down the vertical leg of Pinkerton's *P*. In addition, she served as a Spanish tutor in her senior year and was active in the school chapter of Students Against Drunk Driving.

The only indication in those times that Pam might possibly have been deviating from the norm—and it certainly did not appear to be serious, considering that practically every other teenage girl in the world had the same feeling—was her obsession with rock music. In the Pinkerton annual, she was quoted as saying her main pursuit in life was to dance the night away with David Lee Roth, who at the time was the lead singer for a heavy-metal band called Van Halen. The difference was, Pam never outgrew the fixation. Later, when she got her own car—a silver Honda CRX—she christened it with a vanity license plate reading "Halen." Also, Halen was the name of her Chinese Shih Tzu, a cuddly, Pekingese-like puppy with long, silky, reddish brown hair and a fluffy tail that curved over its back. In adulthood those two things were to guide her life as much as anything else: unswerving love for rock music and her dog.

Ironically it was her love of rock that made Gregg so attractive to her initially. Eschewing college in favor of entering the work force right out of high school, Gregg was working on a heavy-equipment assembly line, just drifting through life with music and women as his main avocations. His long hair and his happy-go-lucky manner reminded Pam of Jon Bon Jovi, a popular rock star of the day. It may have been a physical attraction as much as anything, but from the night they met, Gregg and Pam became a couple.

After she graduated from Pinkerton, Pam had seen enough of the long gray New England winters, and she began thinking longingly of the Florida sunshine, which she missed terribly. So when it came time for her to pick a college, her choice was definitely not north of the Mason-Dixon line.

Remembering her childhood in Florida, she decided to enroll at Florida State University, located in the state capital, Tallahassee. A former girl's school, FSU has since carved out a sizable niche in the world of collegiate athletics. A longtime admirer of Barbara Walters and other nationally known TV anchorwomen, Pam decided to make broadcasting her career. Surprisingly, although FSU has some five hundred majors in eleven different tracks in its Department of Communications, it does not offer any journalism courses. As a result, Pam picked as her major a rather oddly named field called "media performance," which apparently stresses behavior on camera rather than reportorial skills. That was close enough for her. Intending to forge a career in the public eye (an ambition she eventually would realize in a decidedly contrary way), she jumped into the

FSU life-style as energetically as she did Pinkerton's.

By then, however, she had learned to channel her energies in a more constructive fashion, with an eye toward career advancement. Cheerleading was out; working for the broadcast medium was in. First she went to the director of the FSU student radio station, WVFS-FM, and suggested a special program aimed at students like her who were consumed with a passion for hard rock. The manager was so impressed with her drive that he gave her her own one-night-a-week show that she called "Metal Madness." She billed herself as the "Maiden of Metal."

She also worked as an intern at the local CBS affiliate, WCTV, although her duties there consisted of little more than answering telephones in the odd hours. Indefatigable, she also had a third job, as an errand girl with the Bureau of Economic Analysis. In her spare time she organized a benefit at a Tallahassee American Legion Hall promoting safe sex and convinced several bands from the area to give free performances.

Far from neglecting her classwork for her jobs, she was an academic leader. When she received her BA in communications in August 1988—having completed a four-year course in a little more than three years—it was as a cum laude student with a highly respectable 3.85 grade point average.

5

WHEN SHE WASN'T THROWING all her energy into her various school- or job-related activities, Pam was commuting regularly to New England. Her father's airline travel privileges came in very handy, allowing her to fly frequently from Florida to New Hampshire so she could spend time with Gregg. Eventually, however, the love-by-long-distance arrangement grew wearisome, so they decided to cut down on the travel. Since Gregg had no job and no studies to keep him in New Hampshire, he moved to Tallahassee.

When it came time for him to go, William and Judith helped him pack the Mercury Cougar he owned at the time. Then they filled their Toyota with what was left and followed him south. In Tallahassee, Judith went shopping for the basics he and Pam would need to set up an apartment. And then she helped him decorate his new place.

Once he got settled, Gregg took a job with a landscaping company while Pam concentrated on completing her work toward a degree.

According to what friends later told reporters, Pam and Gregg got along divinely. In January Gregg withdrew the small amount of savings he had been able to set aside and bought a modest diamond ring for Pam. Early that year he proposed to her, and she happily accepted.

At about that time a cloud began forming on the horizon; Gregg began to grow up. Realizing that his future was limited without a more focused goal, he decided to become an insurance salesman like his father. To reach that goal he had to begin doing something he thought he had left behind forever: studying. While Pam was knocking herself out, as usual, with her flurry of activities, Gregg was spending his spare time studying to pass the exam he would have to clear if he wanted to sell insurance. He made it.

As Pam's graduation date drew closer, they began discussing what they would do after FSU. Gregg, who missed the snow and the skiing, wanted to return to New Hampshire. Pam, who loved the sun, wanted to stay in Florida. Surprisingly, in the end it was Pam who surrendered. After she graduated they packed up and headed north with their family-to-be increased by one, the addition of the puppy, Halen, who had been a graduation present from Gregg.

Once back in New Hampshire, they moved into the rented condo on Misty Morning Drive. It was only a block from Gregg's parents' home and less than a five-minute walk from Pam's old high school, Pinkerton Academy. They furnished their new home with contemporary furniture, including a white leather couch that Pam thought was the epitome of interior decoration and comfort.

Although Pam knew that Gregg was going to sign on as a salesman trainee with the same company that his father had worked for all his life, Metropolitan Life of Nashua, the shocker came when Gregg cut his hair. To Pam that was a major turning point in their relationship. Instead of Bon Jovi, Gregg, with his shorn locks, looked like just another New England yuppie.

Despite the shock this caused her, they went ahead with their wedding plans. On May 7, 1990, when Gregg was twenty-four and Pam twenty-two, they were married in a large ceremony at Sacred Heart Catholic Church in Lowell, Massachusetts, just over the state line. Fifty-one weeks later Gregg was murdered.

Gregg, who up until then had seemed so ambitionless, dived into insurance sales as enthusiastically as Pam had done with her activities at Pinkerton and FSU. He turned into such an aggressive peddler that he was named Metropolitan's 1990 Rookie of the Year for his New Hampshire district.

Possibly to set an example for his potential customers, Gregg was one of his own good customers. He and Pam had hardly settled in when he bought two policies on his own life, totaling $140,000.

Setting her eye on media work, Pam applied for a job in the newsroom at the state's largest and most influential TV station, WMUR in Manchester, an ABC affiliate. Because she had no professional credentials, the station turned her down, suggesting she get some experience and try again. Instead she took a job as media services director with the school board in the town of Hampton, which was near the coast south of Portsmouth.

Taking the job meant a forty-five-minute commute for her each way from Derry, but it was a start, and the one thing Pam had never lacked was determination. Besides, the position was not without responsibility. She had her own office in a small building across the parking lot from Winnacunnet High School, a rambling series of red brick buildings on Alumni Drive, just off Highway 51. Although the neighborhood now is a middle-class residential area, for 160 years, beginning in 1638, it was the town center. A placard near the school identifies the area as what once was called Winnacunnet Plantation and details how a nearby street, Landing Road, was the thoroughfare carved out of what was then a wilderness by one of the town's founders, the Reverend Stephen Bachiler, in order to move goods inland from the original port.

As media services director, Pam was responsible for distributing and producing educational videos for use in the school district. To help her with this task, she had a secretary and a student intern.

In addition, Pam, the quintessential overachiever, also volunteered to serve as an adult facilitator with a local drug awareness program called Project Self-Esteem, which was a mandatory program for all freshmen at Winnacunnet High. There also were student facilitators—upperclassmen who already had been through the program—who worked with the adults. It was this program that would, in the end, lead to most of Pam's troubles.

Despite the impression given in later news reports, Pam was never a teacher. She never held a teaching certificate, and she never faced a class. But then again, she didn't have to do that to establish regular contact with students.

Despite the facade they presented to the world, by late that year, some seven months after they were married, Pam and Gregg were having problems.

Seemingly convinced that her husband was becoming a yuppie, Pam began examining their relationship with fresh eyes. Although he still enjoyed rock music, Gregg's dedication to it was lessening. He had some good equipment, including an expensive set of speakers in his Toyota pickup truck, and he could still enjoy a new album or even one of the oldies, like Van Halen's *1984*, which included a classic called "Hot for Teacher"; but music was no longer a focus of his existence. Instead he was into selling insurance or spending his free time with his buddies.

On weekends he and some friends would meet

at Windham Depot and go barreling off into the woods on their four-wheelers. Or he would go skiing with his friends rather than his wife. And when he was in the mood to listen to music, he would more frequently drive to Boston to catch his friends from the old days who were performing with regional bands.

Gregg never mentioned his marital problems to his parents. On the contrary, he told them that his plans for the immediate future included buying a real house instead of a condo and settling down like the people he worked with. He was even beginning to think about raising a family, he said. But first he had to convince Pam, and he knew that would not be easy.

Complicating the situation was the fact that maybe he was developing a roving eye. While he was out of town on a business trip in December, he met another woman, and the two ended up in bed together. It was a one-nighter, an affair that meant nothing emotionally to either Gregg or the woman. But it apparently ate at his conscience. Not long afterward he confessed his indiscretion to Pam.

That, according to a friend in whom he eventually confided, was a big mistake. From what Gregg said, Pam was far from understanding about his lapse, and every time they got into an argument—which was happening with considerable regularity as 1990 dawned—she would bring up his affair.

6

ON THE OTHER HAND, Pam herself was not behaving with absolute marital steadfastness. As part of her job and her work with the drug awareness program, she had been thrown into close contact with one of the student facilitators, a shy-looking fifteen-year-old who bore a remarkable resemblance to the young Paul McCartney. He had long hair tumbling to his shoulders and the kind of big, round, sad eyes you see on those children painted on coffee cups and swatches of velvet. He played the guitar, too, and was absolutely, thoroughly dedicated to rock music, specifically heavy metal. Van Halen was okay, he admitted to Pam, but his real admiration was for another group called Mötley Crüe. The student's name was William Flynn. His family and friends called him Bill or Billy.

Up to that point, life had not been particularly kind to Bill. In 1987, when Pam and Gregg were just beginning their romance, Bill and his parents moved to Seabrook from California. Right away that put him at a mild disadvantage.

Seabrook is primarily a blue-collar town, and its residents are known to those from other areas of the state as "Brookies," a derisive term loosely translated to mean people of low class or people from the wrong side of the track. Brookies generally are regarded by other New Hampshirites with the same disdain that Bostonians reserve for the rest of the world.

Not long after his family made the transition, Bill's father, part owner of a small construction company, was killed in an auto accident, and his mother, Elaine, was left to raise her son alone. She did this by taking a job with a maid service and by working part-time at a modeling agency.

Because she was busy most of her waking moments, Elaine had little time to supervise her son's activities. As a result, he was free at age twelve to roam with his newfound friends, Vance "J.R." Lattime, Jr., and Patrick "Pete" Randall. Over the years they became especially close and were known as the Three Musketeers. They had a reputation for always being ready to help a neighbor by running errands, shoveling snow, or handling odd jobs. If the neighbor was elderly, they either did not charge for their services or they gave a large discount. By a few months, Bill was the youngest of the three.

J.R., whose nickname derived from the fact that he was a junior, had dark curly hair and a long thin face. He also wore thick glasses, which gave him a studious look, apparently a deserved coincidence. His pride, next to the old Camaro he was reworking, was a book collection. His most prized volume: an anthology of Edgar Allan Poe. His ambition, at age fifteen, was to become a marine.

When he wasn't in school or hanging out with his friends, J.R. spent a lot of time with his grandmother in Haverhill, Massachusetts. Sometimes he would go with her to help serve holiday dinners to the unfortunate at the local Presbyterian church.

J.R. and his family—his father, Vance senior, a laborer at the Seabrook nuclear power plant, and his mother, Diane, a clerk at an automobile dealership in nearby Exeter—lived in a converted mobile home, which eventually evolved into the place where Bill, Pete, and J.R. gathered.

By all accounts the Lattimes were generous with their time and space. They took in another teenager, a youth about the same age as J.R. named Ralph Welch.

Before he moved in with the Lattimes, Ralph lived with his father in a shack so disreputable that plastic bags were used for windowpanes. Disgusted with his way of life, Ralph dropped out of school and seemed headed nowhere. J.R.'s mother, who had befriended Ralph's mother, offered Ralph a place to live and talked him into going back to school. Although Ralph was about the same age as J.R. and thought of him as a brother, he was not as close to him as were Bill and Pete, and he did not seem to move in the same social circles; apparently he had little if any contact with Pam Smart.

Pete, a short, athletic-looking youth, was the son of a fisherman and a convenience store clerk. According to his mother, Pete had always been an affectionate son, the kind of youth who always hugged both his parents whenever he left the house whether his friends were there or not.

Of the three, however, he seemed the most likely candidate to end up on the opposite side of the law. He had a history of truancy at Winnacunnet High, one so severe that he was required to repeat his freshman year while his friends moved on to be sophomores. On the other hand, one of his teachers was quoted in a local newspaper as saying that Pete and his two friends—Bill and J.R.—were "impressive" young men.

"Billy was a genuinely likable and caring kid," said the unidentified teacher, "and the other two were intelligent beyond their years."

Pete once confided to a friend—maybe he was joking and maybe not—that his ambition was to be a professional hit man.

Two other major players in the group that eventually would be tied indelibly to Pam were Cecelia Pierce and Raymond "Rayme" Fowler.

Cecelia was Pam's intern in the media services office. A fresh-looking but overweight fifteen-year-old with blond hair and blue eyes, Cecelia became very close to Pam in the months she worked for her and considered her a contemporary rather than an employer. To Cecelia, Pam was someone to hang out with, look up to, and confide in.

Cecelia, however, did not move in the same circles as Bill, Pete, and J.R., and her only contact with them was through Pam.

Rayme, who was older than the other youths by almost two years, had been friends with Pete and J.R. since they were ten or eleven. He was not one of the inner circle, but Bill, J.R., and Pete valued his advice, probably because he was older and considered more worldly.

It is not known whether and to what extent Bill, Pete and J.R. were involved in criminal activity up to the time they came into Pam's sphere. Because they were juveniles, all their records are sealed.

In a deposition taken on February 7, 1991, J.R. refused to answer questions about his involvement in the theft of car radios. Similarly, when Bill was asked about use and possession of non-prescription drugs and theft, he also sought protection behind the Fifth Amendment.

On the other hand, when Pete was questioned about criminal activity, he admitted to using cocaine.

There were no indications, however, that drugs played any role in the events that took place in the winter and spring of 1990. Pete, Bill and J.R. managed to get into enough trouble on their own without resorting to chemical abuse.

7

PAM MET BILL IN THE FALL OF 1989 through Project Self-Esteem. Pam had just started working for the school district—School Administrative Unit 21—and Bill was beginning his sophomore year at Winnacunnet High. She was just a little over twenty-two and married; he was fifteen and a virgin. Surprisingly, it took some four months for the sexual union to be consummated.

In the meantime, as the days ticked by from Indian Summer to dead winter, Pam grew closer both to Bill and Cecelia. In those days J.R. was just along for the ride, and Pete hardly fit into the equation at all. In fact, Pete didn't much care for Pam and expressed this sentiment to Bill on several occasions. It was a comment not well received.

For reasons still not totally understood—presumably because she simply enjoyed their company—Pam got into the habit of escorting Cecelia, Bill, and sometimes J.R. up and down the coastal teenage haunts, from shopping malls, to beachfront arcades, to clubs, to pizza parlors and ice-cream huts. Usually she was the one doing the driving because Bill was not old enough to own a license, much less a car. Sometimes it got very cramped in her little Honda two-seater. While Gregg was off hiking and woods-running with *his* friends, Pam was off with *hers*. Except hers at that stage of her life consisted almost exclusively of the students from Winnacunnet High, all of them half a dozen years her junior.

When Project Self-Esteem failed to offer Pam enough of an occasion to see Bill, to whom she had taken a strong but so far sexually abstemious liking, she got him involved in helping her produce an orange juice commercial she planned to enter in a nationwide contest. When she felt the need to see him, she usually could find an excuse.

On the homefront, things were not improving. At Christmastime, when Gregg confessed his dalliance, it hardly sent Pam into a spasm of commiseration. If anything, it encouraged her to see even more of her young friends.

The relationship with Bill reached a turning point early in February when one gray afternoon Pam found herself alone with the teenager in her office across from the high school.

"Do you ever think about me when I'm not around?" she asked him.

A flabbergasted Bill, who probably had been

thinking of little else in the heat of the normal teenage hormone rush, stammered a reply. "Yeah," he mumbled.

"Well, I think about you all the time," Pam smiled, watching his expression change from confusion to embarrassment to excitement.

From then on it was only a matter of time until the relationship could be consummated. The occasion came not long afterward, on the day after Valentine's Day. Gregg was going to be out of state for an insurance meeting, so Pam arranged to take Bill and Cecelia back to her condo after school to help her get through the lonely hours. On the way to Misty Morning Drive, they stopped at a video store and picked up a stack of movies, including the steamer *9 1/2 Weeks*.

As the three of them sat on Pam's white leather couch watching Kim Basinger and Mickey Rourke engage in sexual acrobatics, the temperature in the room rose considerably.

"Why don't you come upstairs and give me a hand?" Pam said to Bill about halfway through the movie. Trotting up the stairs, they left Cecelia to deal with the stack of videos.

Pam led Bill into the bedroom she shared with Gregg and put a Van Halen CD on the player. Then she excused herself and disappeared into the bathroom.

When she came out five minutes later she was wearing a turquoise negligee she had bought especially for the occasion. Then she punched a few buttons on the CD player and walked to the center of the room. What poured forth at high volume was a Van Halen album named *OU812* ("Oh, you ate one, too"), a disc described by *Rolling Stone* magazine as a musical collection dealing with, as the venerable rock periodical put it, "nothing more complicated than the horizontal rumba."

When the steady beat of Pam's favorite selection from the album began reverberating off the bedroom walls, she started taking off the negligee. The song, "Black and Blue", was by vocalist Sammy Hagar, who had replaced Pam's dream man, David Lee Roth, as the group's main singer. It left little to the imagination. Unlike Roth, who was described by *Rolling Stone* as "a master of sexual punning and wink-wink-nudge-nudge innuendo," Hagar was about as unsubtle as one could be. "When [Hagar] bellows, 'Slip 'n' slide, push it in,' in the unrepentantly raunchy 'Black and Blue,'" the magazine said, "you can bet he's not singing about changing the oil filter in his car."

Pam wasn't interested in oil filters, either. With increasing frenzy she undid the buttons on the negligee one by one, while Bill sat there goggle-eyed. When the song ended, the negligee ended up in a pile on the floor. So did Pam and Bill.

Two and a half hours later, with the movie long over, Cecelia decided to check out the upstairs.

"Hope you guys have your clothes on," she cried out on the way up. They didn't. They were still on the floor.

Blushing, Cecelia retraced her steps down the stairs and began flipping through the channels. Upstairs, as Bill said later, "we had sex everywhere that night. On the floor . . . on the bed . . . everywhere."

That was Bill's sexual initiation. The next morning, as Pam was driving them both to school, he got the second half of the lesson, an initiation into the world of cynicism.

"Last night was great," Pam said, "but we can't keep on like that."

"Why not?" he wanted to know.

"Because of Gregg. If you want to keep seeing me, you're going to have to get rid of my husband."

It was a theme that would be repeated again and again in the coming weeks. Pam and Bill slipped away every chance they could for sex. They made love in the back of her Honda, in the woods, on the ground, standing up, lying down, in a camper parked outside J.R.'s house, even in Bill's room at home, sometimes when his mother was behind a closed door just a few feet away. Four to seven times a day, whenever they could. And just about every time, when they paused for breath, Pam continued to hammer at Bill. "You have to get rid of Gregg," she said. "Otherwise we can't keep on seeing each other."

Why couldn't she simply get a divorce? he asked.

Because he would never leave me alone, she replied. He would follow me everywhere; I'd never be able to have a boyfriend. Besides, she added, if we got a divorce he would get the house, the furniture, and everything, even the dog. "I'd never be able to live without Halen," she added.

When he asked why she didn't love her husband anymore, Pam replied that he abused her and that he was seeing other women.

Bill was hooked, and he knew it. He was addicted to the plentiful and pleasurable sex she provided, and as long as he could put her off about actually *doing* something about Gregg, he was a step ahead of the game.

At the same time, he knew in his gut that it couldn't last forever; he was either going to have to give her up or accede to her wishes about Gregg.

The first real showdown came in April. Earlier, in March, he had promised her he would take care of Gregg, but he hadn't really meant it and his promises never amounted to anything.

She kept insisting until he knew he was going to have to do something.

He couldn't handle it by himself, he argued.

Then get someone to help you, she countered.

I don't have a car, he said; no way to get to the condo.

You can use my car, she responded.

Bill sighed. Okay, he said.

According to Bill, he was able to line up Raymond Fowler as a would-be co-killer. To sweeten the offer, Pam told Bill to tell him he could take whatever he wanted from the condo.

The plan was for Rayme and Bill to pick up Pam's car, drive to the condo, and wait for Gregg to come home. Then the two of them would dispatch him.

Rayme admits agreeing to join Bill, but says all he intended was a burglary, not a murder.

When Bill and Rayme appeared at the designated point, Pam's car was there as promised with the keys in the ignition. Bill slid behind the wheel and turned the key. When he did, the dashboard cassette player kicked on. Pam had left a tape in the player and it was cued to a certain song, *their* song. As he sat there dumbfounded, Sammy Hagar screamed at him:

> *Let's do it 'til we're*
> *black and blue . . .*

It was too much for Bill; he wanted to scream. Instead he deliberately fouled the plan. Taking his time driving to Misty Morning Drive, he went down one wrong street after another. Finally, when he got to the condo, the lights were blazing inside and he knew that Gregg was already home.

Sighing in relief, he returned Pam's car, telling

her he had gotten lost on the way and had arrived too late.

She was not pleased. "You don't love me!" she screamed at him as they sat in her car overlooking the ocean. "You got lost on purpose. If you loved me, you'd do this so you could be with me."

Bill swallowed hard. He knew his delaying tactic had been just that—that Pam would give him no rest until he did what she wanted.

Dejected, he turned to his friends, J.R. and Pete, explaining the situation in detail.

"I felt we had to help him," Pete explained later. "He had already screwed it up . . . so I figured he wasn't doing something right."

8

WITH THE FORMAL ARRIVAL of spring, the plan to kill Gregg Smart moved into high gear.

"After he kept on about it for a couple of weeks, I knew he was serious," Pete said, referring to Bill's obsession with the subject. "Just about every day he'd talk about it, and he finally convinced me that he was going to go through with it. I knew he was serious and there was no way I was going to be able to talk him out of it."

As a friend, Pete said, the least he could do was offer to help, thereby perhaps maximizing the chance they could get away with it.

An influencing factor, he admitted, was Bill's contention that Pam would pay $500 to whoever participated. Ostensibly the money would come out of the $140,000 in insurance money she would collect after Gregg's death.

Also in on the plan was J.R., who would furnish the car, which he would borrow from his grandmother, and the weapon.

Finally, late in April, a date was set. Bill told

his friends that Pam had decided upon May 1 because she knew that Gregg would be working late that night. Plus she had a school board meeting, which would give her an excuse for not being at home.

According to the plan, Pam would leave a door open for Bill and Pete, who would ransack the place to give the impression that the crime was committed by burglars.

They could take whatever they wanted from the condo, Bill relayed, including electronic equipment and jewelry. But there were three prohibitions they must follow:

- Don't turn on any lights. "Pam says Gregg is a real wimp—if he sees a light on, he won't come inside," said Bill.
- Don't hurt the dog. Put him in the basement so he doesn't have to witness the murder. "She doesn't want Halen to be traumatized."
- Use a gun rather than a knife because a knife is too messy. "She doesn't want blood all over the white leather couch."

The plan ran into a slight snag on the afternoon of May 1. When Bill and Pete met at J.R.'s house after school, J.R.'s grandmother's car was not there. She had been unable to deliver it, J.R. said, so they would have to drive to Haverhill to pick it up.

No problem, said Bill, dialing Pam to come get them.

When Pam arrived at J.R.'s house in her CRX,

she and Bill climbed into the back. Since that model had no rear seats, they reclined with their heads at the back of the car and their feet between the driver and the passenger. Although Pam had told them to take all the jewelry in the condo, she had taken steps to make sure they didn't get the better pieces. She had a ring on every finger and gold chains draped around her neck.

J.R. drove and Pete rode in the passenger seat.

Since J.R. had a heavy foot, Pete had to remind him to slow down as they barreled across I-95. The last thing they wanted was to get stopped for speeding and have Bill discovered with a pistol sticking in his belt.

On the twenty-minute drive they went over the plan yet again. Pam reminded them about the dog and the gun, although Pete mentally discounted her admonitions about the firearm. He feared the gun would make too much noise, and since it belonged to J.R.'s father and they would have to return it, there was too much chance of it being traced. He could care less if they got blood on the couch. When it came down to it, though, he was unable to use the knife and Bill had to pull the revolver.

And don't forget, Pam added, wear only clothes that can be thrown away afterward, and make sure your hands are protected so there won't be any incriminating fingerprints.

There was one more thing that had to be

decided: "How should I act when I get home?" she asked, speaking to no one in particular.

J.R. looked at Pete, who turned on the seat to look at Bill. They shrugged.

"I mean it," Pam said. "What should I do? Should I scream? Should I run from house to house? Should I call the police?"

J.R. shrugged again. "Just act normal," he advised.

From Haverhill they returned to Seabrook, where Pam dropped Bill off and returned to her office in Hampton, a short drive away.

J.R. and Pete picked up Rayme and Bill, who had stopped at home to get a duffel bag packed with the sweat suits, sneakers, and gloves. Again, Rayme admits he was there, but says he thought it was only a burglary. With J.R. at the wheel, they drove to Derry and parked at Hood Plaza Center, which was almost across the street from Derry police headquarters.

While waiting for it to get dark, they bought Scotch tape at a nearby grocery and dined on pizza at Papa Gino's.

At dusk, Pete and Bill went to the rear of the shopping center and changed into the sweat suits and old sneakers. While walking up the road to the Smart condominium, they met another group of strollers, so they broke into a trot, pretending to be runners out for an early evening workout.

They jogged around the complex and

approached unit 4E from the rear. They had to wait about ten minutes, huddling in the shadow of the building, while residents of another condo unloaded their car and went inside.

Once the coast was clear, they entered through the cellar door, called a "bulkhead" in New Hampshire, and put the next phase of the plan into operation.

The first task was capturing Halen.

The dog, apparently upset by the unexpected entrance of two strangers, barked and growled. Bill chased him around the couch a couple of times before he could collar him and put him in the cellar.

Pete, who had watched the pursuit with amused interest, climbed the stairs and entered the master bedroom suite, where he dumped the contents of Pam's jewelry box into a pillowcase from the bed. Adding CDs from a player and rack in the bedroom, he helped Bill empty bureau and dresser drawers to give the place a searched-through look, as if a burglar had been looking for other hidden valuables.

At eight-fifteen they went downstairs. Unhappy with the baby blue pillowcase from the bed, which he considered too bright and too feminine, Pete slit open a throw pillow that was on the couch and transferred the jewelry and CDs to it, discarding the other cover. They settled down to wait for Gregg.

Nearby, J.R. and Rayme killed time by changing the oil in J.R.'s grandmother's car and listening to the radio.

Finally, when J.R. saw his two friends approaching at a run across the field that separated the shopping area from the condo complex, he started the car and sped to pick them up.

When they returned to Seabrook, they split up and returned to their own homes, where they acted as if nothing untoward had occurred.

According to J.R., Rayme cleaned the pistol and gave it to J.R., who slipped it back into his father's collection.

On the surface, everything was copacetic.

When Bill reported to her, Pam was delighted with the developments. Her lover and his friend had left nothing behind in the condo to tie them to the murder. She was securely alibied and there had been no witnesses. It had all the elements, Pam bragged, of the perfect crime.

Except for one thing, they might have gotten away with it: somebody talked.

As it turned out, it was somebod*ies*, including Pam, who, more than anyone else, helped seal her own fate. But in the short run, it looked as though they might escape undetected.

9

IN THE DAYS immediately following Gregg's murder, things progressed almost as normal for Pam and the young killers.

Almost immediately, one of the companies with which Gregg had life insurance paid Pam $90,000, which she proceeded to work through fairly rapidly. Within a month she had spent half of it, mostly on a new condo in Hampton, not far from Winnacunnet High, clothes, and furniture. Ironically her prized white leather couch had been ruined in the crime, not by Gregg's blood, as she had feared, but by black powder spread by police in an attempt to find a set of usable fingerprints. But Gregg and Pam's household insurer—in a claim expedited by Bill's father—replaced it.

Significantly, none of her newfound wealth went to J.R. or Pete in compensation for their services. That is not to say they got nothing, however. Pete traded the jewelry he had taken from the condo (most of it was inexpensive gold plate) for cocaine, and J.R., weary of waiting for payment, was given the speakers from Gregg's truck, telling Pam he would credit her with half his promised fee. It was never determined how much money Bill had taken from Gregg's wallet or what happened to it, although he apparently kept it without sharing.

Throughout the month of May, Pam continued seeing Bill. As far as they were concerned, the affair could proceed at its customary torrid, not to mention tawdry, pace.

For the others—J.R., Rayme, Pete, and Cecelia (who had not taken part in the crime but had knowledge of it)—life also went on as usual, with one big difference: all of them were privy to a deep, dark secret. The odds were overwhelming that sooner or later the word was going to leak out. The only really surprising part was that it took as long as it did.

Hampered by an almost total absence of physical evidence, investigators were running in circles trying to get a strong lead. The only real contact they had at that time was with Pam, and her story was virtually unshakable. She had been at a school board meeting (which had been easy enough to verify), and she had returned home to find her husband dead. The coroner's report firmly fixed the time of death at 8:30–9:00 P.M. on May 1, and it would have been impossible for her to have left her meeting, driven to Derry to shoot her husband, and get back to the meeting without being missed. It was a thirty- to forty-five-minute drive each way from Derry to Hampton.

Besides, it was difficult to cast an undue amount of suspicion on Pam. Within hours of the murder she had volunteered to be interviewed by local media to appeal for help in finding whoever had committed the crime. At FSU she had been trained in media performance, and in May 1990 she was showing the results of that training. She came across as a highly credible, totally sympathetic victim.

Although police were 90 percent certain the murder *was not* part of an aborted burglary, as it was made to appear, they had nothing to indicate what it *was*. Investigators may have been convinced that Pam was the key to the puzzle, but until they had more to go on there was nothing they could do.

That was not to say that Pam was endearing herself to the Derry police. Apparently they were as tight-lipped with her as they were with reporters, and her frequent—sometimes angry—calls to them demanding information failed to make her lots of friends in the cop shop. She was, however, just as demanding of others connected with the case. After the murder Pam initiated a determined telephone campaign to talk to just about anyone who might have been questioned by investigators to see what *they* knew, on the off chance it might give her some insight into how the investigation was progressing. But because the police actually had so few leads, it was an exercise in futility on Pam's part.

From the beginning, though, it was almost inevitable the front put up by Pam and the youths would eventually break. In mid-May, some two weeks after the murder, the wall began to crack. Just where those first leaks came from has never been publicly disclosed. But sources close to the investigation have said the reports at first came in anonymously. They did not give the full details of the plot but merely hinted that Pam may have had something to do with her husband's death. They were on the order of statements like "Look more closely at Pam" or "Pam isn't telling you all she knows."

Despite these tantalizing tidbits, investigators still were unable to make any significant headway. Apparently they did not even know of the existence of Bill, Pete, J.R., or Rayme, but they did know that Cecelia was close to Pam. During May they interviewed her several times, but she always denied that she was the one providing the early information. Later she would play a momentous role in the case, but other developments had to occur first.

The investigators' first big break came early in June, and it arrived completely out of the blue. It came from Ralph Welch, the teenager who had been given shelter with J.R.'s family.

On Saturday, June 9, Ralph went to J.R. and

Pete, who were sitting in J.R.'s room. "Is it true what I've heard?" he asked. "That you guys had something to do with a murder?"

The two appeared surprised and quickly denied any involvement. Pretending to be relieved at their denial, Ralph left the room. But instead of returning to his own quarters, he retraced his steps and stood outside J.R.'s room, eavesdropping.

What he heard was J.R. whisper, "Jesus, Bill's going to be pissed. And you know who's going to be next."

Interpreting that to be confirmation of the rumor—and assuming that the "next" was going to be his cousin, Rayme, who Pete and J.R. suspected was the source of the rumor—Ralph ran back into the room. Jumping on Pete, whom he had known since the first grade, Ralph started screaming, "I heard you! I heard you! Now tell me."

"Shhhhhh," J.R. cautioned. "You're going to wake everybody up."

"Tell me!" Ralph insisted.

"Okay, okay," said Pete, extricating himself from beneath his old friend. "But let's go outside. I don't want Diane to wake up and have to go to the bathroom and hear us talking about this."

Ralph agreed. As he and Pete stood under the trees at midnight, Pete outlined the tale, explaining what had happened and why. It took him about thirty minutes to give Ralph the short version.

When he finished, Ralph was pale and his eyes were frightened. "I can't believe you did that," he said. "That you actually killed somebody."

"Why not?" Pete replied. That's what they do in the army. They do it every day."

"But *you're* not in the army," Ralph insisted. "How could *you* do it?"

Pete grinned. "Who knows?" he said. "Maybe I want to be a hired assassin."

A worried look crossed Ralph's face. "Does that mean you're going to get me now?" he asked.

"No," Pete assured him. "Why would we do that?"

Soon afterward Pete left to return to his own house, but on his way back to J.R.'s the next morning, Ralph met him in the driveway.

"I don't want you to come around here anymore," he said.

Surprised, Pete just stared at him.

"Are you going to make me stay away?" Pete asked.

"Yeah, I am," said Ralph, swinging on his friend.

Pete threw an arm around him, and they wrestled on the ground for about ten minutes before J.R. pulled them apart.

"Come on," J.R. said, "this isn't solving anything."

As Ralph walked back into the house, Pete and J.R. climbed aboard J.R.'s road bike and roared off to Pam's condo, where they knew they would find both Pam and Bill.

"We've got a serious problem," Pete said as soon as he and J.R. were ushered inside.

Whatever Pam and the others planned, it was too late for damage control.

While the group was meeting in Pam's condo, Ralph was huddled with J.R.'s father, explaining to him all that he had discovered in the last twelve hours. When he finished, Vance Lattime went to the cabinet where he kept his guns and removed the .38-caliber Charter Arms revolver that had been used to kill Gregg. He pocketed the weapon, then he and Ralph got in the car and went to the Seabrook police, where they repeated the story and turned over the pistol.

The next day, Monday, June 11, Bill, Pete and J.R. were picked up as they were leaving a movie theater after watching Arnold Schwarzenegger's *Total Recall*. Pam was not arrested. Not then.

10

NOT SURPRISINGLY, the arrests were big news in New Hampshire.

The Nashua *Telegraph* put the story in its lead spot in the upper right hand corner just below the flag. The main headline read THREE JUVE-NILES ARRESTED IN DERRY DEATH, and carried the subhead "AG May Try Them as Adults in Shooting of Gregory Smart."

The story, by Steve Ericson, thanks to the Derry Police Department's no-tell policy, gave few details other than the fact that an arrest had taken place. Because Pete, Bill, and J.R. were only sixteen, their names were not disclosed, nor were any details of where they had been arrested or why.

"Neither [police] nor [the attorney general's spokeswoman] would answer questions pertaining to a motive in the shooting, nor would they say whether there had been threats against Smart or his family," the story said. It added that the three would be arraigned at a "closed session" on Tuesday.

In its early edition, the Manchester *Union Leader* also gave front-page play to the story of the arrests, but not in the same favored position as the *Telegraph*. The headline in the Manchester newspaper read THREE ARRESTED IN GREG [SIC] SMART MURDER CASE, and was subheaded, "Juveniles Facing Court in May Slaying in Derry." That version of the story, which was not bylined, had even less information than the *Telegraph*'s. However, in a later edition the newspaper said the youths were sixteen and seventeen years old and attended Winnacunnet High. It also made the transition by pointing out that Pam was employed by the school district that included the high school the youths attended.

The following day's *Telegraph* reported that two of the youths (it did not say which two) had been arraigned, but the hearing for the third had been postponed. It added new information that a gun also had been recovered, but the reporter, Ericson, was unable to get confirmation that it was the gun that had killed Gregg.

That day's story also introduced Diane Nicolosi, an assistant attorney general who later would play a prominent role in the case. Mostly, though, it quoted her as refusing to comment.

The *Union Leader*, which had scored a point by being first to tie the youths to Winnacunnet and Pam, struck again in its June 13 state edition. With a story taking up two-thirds of the top of the front page, the *UL* screamed STATE WANTS YOUTHS TRIED AS ADULTS IN DERRY MURDER. Other than specifying that an adult convicted of first-degree murder or accomplice to first-degree murder faced a sentence of life without parole, it had little new information.

On June 14 the *Union Leader* again took up a large chunk of the top one-third of its front page with a story by Michael Cousineau and Tami Plyler. It contained the interesting information that in addition to the three already in custody, another arrest was expected. Although it still did not cite Bill, J.R., or Pete by name, it carried their pictures: thumbnail-size portraits under the general heading ARRAIGNED. The caption said only, "These three Seabrook juveniles were arraigned this week in connection with the Derry shooting." Even more interesting, a photo of Pam accompanied the story, except it was on an inside page. It, too, was a thumbnail-size reproduction and was captioned simply with her name and the notation "Victim's widow."

From what was testified to later, there is no doubt that these developments had a profound effect upon Pam. On the day the *Union Leader* published the pictures of Bill, Pete, and J.R.—and Pam—she issued a position statement. "I want to be happy because they caught someone," she said, "but I don't have enough information in my own mind that they are guilty."

She was right about one thing: she did not have enough information. Since police refused to discuss any details with her, she went into a new phone frenzy, calling anyone who might have some connection with the investigation to pump them for details. She wound up with nothing.

But had she known about one other event that occurred that day, she really would have panicked.

About the time Pam was talking to the press, Cecelia, her loyal intern, also was talking: to the police.

Under heavy pressure for many weeks—from the police, from Pam, from her peers—Cecelia, whatever her reasons, decided she had had enough. Asking for a session with Derry Police Captain Loring Jackson, Cecelia spilled what she knew. Even more important, she agreed to help police get the goods on her friend and mentor. When asked by Jackson if she would be willing to have future conversations with Pam taped, Cecelia readily agreed. The first test came a mere five days later, on June 19. On that day Cecelia had two telephone conversations with Pam, both of which were recorded by investigators.

The equipment used by Derry police was incredibly primitive, and the resulting tapes had to be enhanced electronically to make them as clear as possible. But the tale they presented was remarkable, both for its audacity and for its insight into Pam's thought process. Later, investigators would get even more daring—and put their imformant at even greater risk—by outfitting Cecelia with a body mike and sending her to talk to Pam face to face. But the June 19 tapes were exceptional in their own right.

The first tape began with Cecelia calling Pam's office at five minutes before three on that Tuesday afternoon.

Getting right to the point, Cecelia told Pam that investigators from Derry had gotten in touch with her on their car phone, saying they were on their way to her house to conduct yet another interview.

"I don't know what to do," Cecelia confessed.

Pam was blasé. "Answer the questions," she said.

"What if they ask me again about you and Bill having an affair? Do you still want me to deny it?" Cecelia asked.

"Well, we weren't."

"No?" Cecelia asked uncertainly.

"Just answer the questions and that's it, you know," said Pam.

"All right," Cecelia agreed.

"You know," Pam continued, "you're not supposed to answer any questions about . . . your opinion. You know, like 'So what did you think of Bill?' or something like that."

"Yeah," Cecelia prompted.

"You're not supposed to answer that 'cause

you're only supposed to answer questions that are fact."

Pam elaborated upon her advice, stressing that Cecelia should refuse to give her opinion to the police about anything.

Trying to get her to open up a bit more, Cecelia added that she also was still getting calls from reporters. She said newsmen from the Lawrence *Eagle-Tribune* had tracked her to the Dunkin' Donuts, where they questioned the workers about her and her classmates.

"But see," Pam said, "that's just [the workers'] *opinions*, though. You know what I mean?"

"Yeah," Cecelia answered hesitantly.

Pam had a new thought. "Is your mom there?" She was not, Cecelia replied.

Obviously that was what Pam was hoping she would say. "I don't know, if I were you, if I would answer *any* questions" without your mother being present, she said. "If [the investigators] make you feel uncomfortable, just tell them you don't want to answer any more questions until your mom gets there."

"Okay," Cecelia said brightly. Then she changed the subject. "I saw [Ralph] on the street yesterday."

"What did he say?" Pam asked.

"I just rode by him," Cecelia said, "but I guess he's going around telling everybody all sorts of stuff."

"Like what?" Pam said, her curiosity piqued.

"Like that you paid the guys a thousand dollars—not apiece, though. I guess he's telling people that you paid them a thousand dollars to split."

"I didn't pay anybody anything," Pam said indignantly. "That's so queer. I didn't do that." Technically she was correct. She had *promised* through Bill to pay them, but she never had.

"And Raymond's going around saying the same thing, saying that you paid them for killing Gregg, but—"

"Well, Raymond's obviously wrong, too," Pam interrupted.

Cecelia asked Pam if she had talked to Bill or his mother, and Pam replied that she had not. "As far as Bill's mom says, he isn't confessing to anything. And even if he does, he'd simply say . . . that he did it and all that."

"Yeah," Cecelia agreed. At that point she decided to push a little harder to get Pam to incriminate herself.

"The only question that [the investigators] really asked about you was they asked me if I thought you knew anything about it before it happened. And I lied, naturally. I said no."

Pam was not to be trapped. "Yeah. Well, I didn't."

"I know," Cecelia responded, "but listen, if they find out that I lied for you, am I going to be charged with—"

Pam interrupted again. "You're not going to be lying for me. You didn't lie about anything. You don't know anything. What the hell's the problem?"

"Okay," Cecelia answered meekly.

"I mean, if someone's saying that you're lying and you're saying that you're not, it's their word against yours and that's it."

"Okay."

"If they ask you to get a lie detector test, which I doubt they will, then you just say you're going to get yourself a lawyer first, and any lawyer will tell you not to."

For the next few minutes Pam spoke elliptically, bouncing from subject to subject. One minute she talked about the orange juice commercial she had produced and WMUR newsman Bill Spencer, who was trying to get a copy of the video; the next she brought up Ralph and Raymond.

"How would Raymond and Ralph know anything?" Pam asked. "Maybe somebody told them that, or somebody else said that they did. You know what I mean? You're not going to get convicted of murder on someone else's opinion."

"I know." Cecelia sighed. "This whole thing is so stupid. I just wish you guys could have just got a divorce instead."

"You wish that what?" Pam asked.

"That you guys just got divorced instead. It would have been so easy."

"Well, anyways," Pam said ruminatively. "All right. I'll just talk to you later, I guess."

* * *

In the next conversation, almost two hours later, Pam began by telling Cecelia that she was sorry for the trouble she was causing her, especially since she was the reason Cecelia was being hounded by reporters. Once they realized that she didn't know anything, they would leave her alone, Pam promised. And the same would be true for the police.

For a woman who wanted to make her career in broadcasting, Pam proved on the tape to be amazingly inarticulate, sprinkling "you know" and "like" and "you know what I mean" after every other phrase. Often she changed thought in midsentence so that it frequently was difficult to follow her exactly. For example, in this passage she apparently is trying to calm Cecelia:

"They'll just leave you alone, too, you know what I mean. They're just doing part of their job and that's just, you know if . . . I don't know what the guys are saying. I doubt, you know, according to Ms. Flynn, like that no one is confessing and that they're all sitting around saying they didn't do it so I mean I'm sure that the police are saying J.R. and Bill said that you did it, you know what I mean, or whatever, you know, and trying to get everyone to confess, but that has nothing to do with you, you're not on trial, you know what I mean?"

Cecelia obviously did *not* know what she meant, but she had a concise answer: "Yeah."

"They're on trial," Pam continued, "and that's it, so you just, you know, answer the questions and that's it. They're going to try and get you to talk and to confess and, you know, they're going to say 'We know you know' and all that, you know, try and make you nervous, but all you have to do is just maintain the same story, you know, and that's it, you know, you don't know and that's it, you know. As far as where you were that night, I would get the story straight, you know, so that they can't get suspicious and wonder where you were and all that, you know. But just answer their questions and don't offer any information, you know."

She also tried to allay Cecelia's fears of being arrested and charged in connection with the murder, bucking her up by telling her that if they were going to arrest her, they probably would have done so already. But it was not difficult to discern that *Pam* was the one who was really worried. At the time, though, she seemed to be more concerned about her affair with Bill being revealed than she was with the possibility that she was being investigated in connection with her husband's murder.

"That's ridiculous," she said, referring to the rumor of the relationship that existed between her and Bill. "Why would I, why would a twenty-two-year-old woman like me, be having an affair with a sixteen-year-old high school student? That's just ridiculous."

She continued for more than a minute, ricocheting from point to point like a pinball, before coming back to the main issue.

"See, Bill had spent a lot of time with me. People might have believed he was in love with me or something like that. But that's only people's opinions, you know what I mean? You can't document the fact that a person is in love with another person."

Finally she sighed in frustration. "I feel like I'm the only one the police aren't asking anything, you know."

11

IT WAS ALMOST A MONTH LATER before investigators made another tape of a Pam/Cecelia conversation. During that month, as was obvious from the recording, the pressure was starting to get to Pam. Being unsure what, if anything, Pete, J.R., and Bill were saying from behind bars was disconcerting enough; equally frustrating was the fact that Pam had no idea how the investigation was progressing. Moreover, the coastal communities were abuzz with rumors and gossip, and even her best friend seemed to be turning against her. When Cecelia showed up unexpectedly at Pam's office on July 12, a rainy, sultry Thursday, she found her friend in a foul mood.

"I was just going to call you," Pam said. "I saw your old boyfriend yesterday."

"Yeah?" Cecelia said noncommittally.

"He told me that you're going around telling everyone that I killed Gregg," Pam said accusingly.

This was not what Cecelia expected. But she decided to see it through.

"He did?"

"I couldn't believe that you would say that. That I actually killed him. That I shot him."

"I did not say that," Cecelia assured her.

"I thought he had the story fucked up," Pam said, softening slightly. "Hug me," she commanded. "I haven't seen you in so long. I missed you."

Cecelia had a moment of panic. What if she felt the mike? But there was no way to get around it. She gave Pam a hug, and then she went on the offensive.

She had seen her old boyfriend, too, she said. And he had told her that Pam had been around looking for her and that she was carrying a knife, which he implied he wanted to use on her, Cecelia.

"*What*?" said a surprised Pam.

"No shit," Cecelia said.

Pam was not to be distracted. Cecelia's old flame, she said, claimed that Cecelia was spreading the rumor that Pam had killed "some guy." He had not, however, said "Gregg" or "her husband."

"He goes 'some guy.' I go, 'What do you mean?' He goes, 'She's going around telling everybody that you murdered *some guy*.' He didn't say anything about Bill or anything else, so I figured he must have gotten the story fucked up."

In any case, Pam added, she was glad Cecelia came in. "I want to talk to you," she said. "My lawyer told me that someday they're probably going to bug you and that you'd come down and talk to me."

Cecelia's heart skipped another couple of beats. "I haven't even talked to the police," she said, praying that she sounded convincing. Trying to change the subject, she blurted out that she had seen Bill's brother and that he didn't seem to be worried that he was facing possible murder charges.

"What is going on?" Pam asked. "Because Ralph—"

Cecelia broke in. "Ralph is telling the whole town everything."

"But Ralph doesn't *know* anything," Pam added.

Cecelia shrugged. "Ralph knows what he heard."

Pam said a reporter had contacted her and said that Ralph claimed she and Bill were having an affair. "But it's not enough to arrest me because of what Ralph heard," she said, more question than statement.

"Right," Cecelia agreed.

"And for all anybody knows Bill could have been totally in love with me and told the whole Winnacunnet [High School] that he was having an affair with me." Just because Ralph heard something, she added, did not mean it was the truth. "If the police believed that, I'd be arrested right now, so obviously they don't believe it."

Cecelia said a reporter from the Derry *News*

had been to her house three times trying to get her to talk about Pam and Bill. But, she added, the reporter thought that Pam was innocent, "so don't worry about her."

"Oh, I'm not worried about *her*," Pam shot back. "I'm not worried about anything except the police. I mean, if Pete or J.R. or Bill says that I did it."

"Right," Cecelia agreed.

"Right," Pam added. "Then they can arrest me."

"Yeah."

"Then I want you to know that if I'm in jail, there's no way in hell I'm ever going to say anything about you. Ever. You didn't have anything to do with anything, and even if they have a phone conversation or something with me and Bill, then I'd have to admit that yes, I was having an affair with Bill. [But] I am never going to admit it. The fact that I asked . . . that I told him that I hired them because I never paid them money. I never hired them."

Cecelia felt her legs go weak. "I know you didn't, but—"

Pam interrupted. "That's the thing. I never fucking paid them. Someone told me I gave J.R. a stereo and stuff [but] that's not true."

Pam made it clear she thought the world was closing in on her. "All I know is that I'm not even really going to talk about it ever again because I think my phone is probably tapped or something. But the thing is, I don't know what Ralph knows because I don't know what they told him."

"Or what he heard."

"Right. But does the whole fucking Seabrook hate me pretty much?"

"Well," Cecelia said, trying to be tactful, "if I was you I wouldn't drive through there."

"I drove through there yesterday," Pam said, not appreciating the effort. "Tell me how the town feels," she said. "Like what do they think? Do they think, like, Pam's a bitch?"

Cecelia laughed. The general feeling, she said, was that Pam had engineered Gregg's murder. Otherwise why would Bill, Pete, and J.R. have done it?

"Even if I asked somebody to kill somebody, you'd have to be fucking deranged to say okay."

"As far as I can see it," Cecelia ventured, "Bill did it because he loved you. I mean, you didn't pay him, right?"

"Right," Pam answered. "I didn't pay anybody."

"*Did* you pay him?" Cecelia pushed.

"No," Pam replied. "That's the thing. But I mean, why would the other people do it? It's not going to make sense in a court of law, right?"

One sign of the tension she was under was Pam's concern—a concern bordering on preoccupation—about what people were saying about her.

"I wonder if everybody hates me at Winnacunnet? Or if they just feel sorry for me? Could be everyone thinks I'm guilty."

"I don't think anybody knows what to think," Cecelia replied, trying to cheer her up.

"Does anybody feel sorry for me?" Pam continued. "Like, is anybody [asking] 'How could they have killed her husband?' Or is it that everybody thinks I had something to do with it?"

Cecelia said she had been told "five times already" that Pam had been arrested.

"So have I," Pam said. "But obviously I'm not. The police haven't even questioned me." She sounded almost regretful, as though she were the only one in the class that hadn't had her picture taken.

Still, in spite of the lack of official investigatory interest, Pam confessed that she felt she needed legal counsel. So she had hired "the best frigging lawyers anywhere."

Cecelia was surprised. "You have?" she asked.

"Yeah," Pam confirmed. "But they're fucking wicked expensive. But what could I do?"

"Obviously you can afford it," Cecelia commented.

"No, goddamn fucking [I can't]. But didn't I need them, you know?"

As part of her growing paranoia, Pam seemed worried that Cecelia was going to go to the police. To ensure that she would not, Pam felt it necessary to lay out the problems that could cause for her friend. When Cecelia told her that an investigator from the attorney general's office—which under New Hampshire law has the authority to handle homicides across the state—was coming to interview her, Pam used the opening to put the fear of God into her.

"I want you to know this and never forget this, okay?"

Cecelia nodded.

"In New Hampshire," Pam explained, "you're not an accessory to murder if you know *after* the fact. You're only an accessory if you know *before* the fact. . . ."

"Right. . . ."

"And if you're part of the planning and execution. Okay?"

"Right," said Cecelia.

"That's why Raymond ended up saying he didn't know anything before," Pam contended.

"Because he wasn't part of the planning?"

"Right," Pam agreed. "[Otherwise] he would be arrested right now." (He would, in fact, later be charged in connection with the murder.)

"So if you know after the fact, you're not an accessory," Pam repeated. "If [police] try to tell you that if you confess . . ."

"Yeah?" Cecelia interjected, all ears.

Pam sighed deeply. "Don't confess, okay?"

"All right," Cecelia agreed.

What an investigator would be telling her would not be true, Pam asserted. "They *will* fucking arrest you and you *will* be an accessory."

Cecelia nodded.

"You *will*," Pam stressed. "No matter what plea-bargaining bullshit they tell you."

Unsure how to react, Cecelia laughed.

"I'm serious," Pam reminded her. "Don't forget [what I've told you] because my lawyer told me that and that's the thing. If J.R. comes forward and says 'If I'm going down, Raymond, so are you' and [he says] that Raymond knew, then Raymond's going to be arrested. Even though he already turned state's evidence, he will be arrested as an accessory."

"I hope he is," Cecelia added. "I hope that if they are found guilty or anything, I hope Raymond goes down with them. He deserves it."

"No shit." Pam sighed.

The conversation veered off temporarily while Cecelia and Pam discussed how Raymond and Ralph were related, but Pam soon steered the talk back to Cecelia's position.

"I'm just telling you," she emphasized to Cecelia in an apparent attempt to ensure her silence, "that if you tell the truth, you're going to be an accessory to murder."

"Right," Cecelia repeated.

"So that's your choice," Pam replied. "Not only [will you be charged], but what is your family going to think? They're going to be, like, 'Cecelia, you knew about this,' you know?"

"Yeah."

"Everybody in town is going to be, like, fucking, you know, Cecelia . . . So if I were you . . . Once you say 'no' they leave you alone. [But] once you say 'yes' they never leave you alone."

12

FEELING THAT THE CONVERSATION was drifting away again, Cecelia tried to pull the talk back to Gregg's murder.

"Seeing what happened," she prompted Pam, "wouldn't you rather have just divorced Gregg?"

"Well, I don't know," Pam said indecisively. "Nothing was going wrong until that fucking Ralph—"

"No shit," Cecelia interrupted, cutting Pam off before she could complete her chain of thought.

"It's their [own] stupid-ass fault," Pam said, trying to regain her thread. "They told Ralph."

"I can't even believe that they told," Cecelia said, feigning sympathy. "Now they're in jail, and every time I hear Mötley Crüe I think of Bill."

"Yeah, so do I," Pam agreed. "Tell me about it."

Cecelia wanted to know when they were going to go "clubbing" again, and that brought the conversation back to Cecelia's former boyfriend, the one who had told her that Pam was looking for her to kill her.

"I don't go out clubbing," Pam said, working up into another feeling-sorry-for-herself-mood. "What the hell, I went out fucking once because everyone's trying to get me to go out. Fucking give me a break. I haven't done a goddamn thing. I sit fucking home and"—sighing—"I don't know what to do. You know what I mean? I feel like shit. But it's not my fault."

Cecelia agreed that her old flame was not a very nice person.

"Yeah," Pam agreed. "That fucking asshole. He told me that you just went down there and made a fucking statement . . . but who gives a shit? He's obviously a dick, you know?"

Cecelia said he told her that Pam was looking for her and she was armed with "a Rambo knife."

"That's so queer." Pam laughed. "Why would I show it to him?" Then, in words that would come back to haunt her, she added: "Obviously you know I would never kill you."

Pam and Cecelia's conversations did not necessarily follow a logical pattern. The talk skipped back and forth among subjects and people, and whatever item was under discussion at any particular time was liable to change with no advance notice. Suddenly, without any apparent reason for swerving, Pam brought up lie detectors again.

"If they ask you to take a lie detector test, try to deal with the questions," she advised.

"Well, I'll just do what you said and change the questions around," Cecelia answered.

"I wouldn't even take it if I were you," Pam suggested.

"I know." Cecelia sighed. "But with my mother there, I really have no choice. My mother's, like, if you're innocent . . ."

"Yeah," Pam agreed. "But if you ask any lawyer in America, the lawyer would tell you not to take it whether you're innocent or not."

"Right."

"That's the thing," Pam continued. "I mean, I don't know anything about lie detector tests, but I know every lawyer I talked to told me no matter fucking what, don't ever in your whole entire life take a lie detector test because they can't even be introduced as evidence, they can only be used against you for further questioning. Like if you show up as you're lying, they're going to fucking bludgeon you to death . . . they're going to question you for ninety hours."

"I know I'll have a nervous breakdown," Cecelia said.

That sent Pam off on another tangent, prompting her to relate how confident she was in her lawyers. "They really got their shit together," she said.

"But you see what I'm saying about accessory before the fact. If they bludgeon you to death for three fucking million hours, and they say to you, 'Well, listen, if you tell the truth . . .'"

Cecelia reminded Pam that she already had been questioned twice, and the last time one of the investigators had hinted that she possibly could be charged with "whatever it's called, hindering evidence—"

"Harboring, or whatever—"

"—whatever it is, he said that I would be in big trouble."

"Not only that," Pam said, trying to add weight to her argument, "but if you confessed right now, they'd rip you apart on the witness stand because they'd be, like, 'Well, Cecelia, before this happened you said you didn't know anything, now all of a sudden you know something.' You're better off," Pam advised, "just to stick with the same fucking story and not know anything, because then they'd finally leave you alone."

Again, the conversation wandered. Cecelia shared with Pam her impressions of an investigator hired by J.R.'s family. "He's good-looking," Cecelia offered, "but I didn't talk to him." Then she added that he implied that she and Pam were having a homosexual relationship.

"Me and you?" Pam asked in astonishment.

"Yeah." Cecelia laughed.

"Naaah." Pam giggled.

"I was laughing so bad," Cecelia said.

"All we did was watch TV," Pam said, referring to the night she'd seduced Bill and left Cecelia watching *9½ Weeks* on the VCR.

"I'm like, 'No, buddy, we're not lesbians. I was sitting downstairs while she was upstairs bopping Bill.'"

"All I can." Pam laughed.

Turning serious again, Pam reminded Cecelia how good she had been to her. "I always thought I was a good friend to you. I let you drive my car and I paid for you, and I took you out, and that was okay because I like being your friend. When this is all over we can still be friends and everything else. I like to think that I've done a lot for you. That's the thing. Even if you send me to the fucking slammer. If anybody sends me, it's going to be you. That's what it comes down to. But what good is it going to do if you send me to the fucking slammer? Because if you think that's going to be the end of your problems . . ."

"I'll be out a pair of sneakers on my next birthday," Cecelia snickered, trying to lighten the mood.

"Don't think that will be the end of your problems," Pam continued, anxious to make her point. "Your whole family is going to be like fucking 'Well, you knew about a murder. How could you have lived like that?' And the newspapers are going to be all over you. 'How could you have known about that?' You know. And you're going to be on the witness stand a million times. He's going to put you on and he'll say, 'Did you know?' And you'll say, 'No.' They're going to ask you, 'Did you work for Pam? Did you stay at her house? What did you guys do?' [And you're going to say], 'We watched a movie.'"

In the end, Pam said, she thought the weak link was J.R. "The only thing that I think is going to happen is that sooner or later J.R. is going to turn on everybody."

Cecelia seemed surprised. "I feel bad for him," she said, "because he really didn't do anything."

"You have to remember," Pam cautioned, "through this whole thing [they] were old enough to make [their] own decisions. They did this all. I did not force anybody to do anything. They made their own decisions."

"At least you didn't pay them," Cecelia added.

"No, I didn't pay them," Pam confirmed. "They made their own decisions. Remember that throughout the whole thing. Don't feel bad even though I do, too. I know it's hard, but remember they made up their own minds. I don't even know what happened in my house. I don't know who was there or who was waiting in the car."

"That's good, though," Cecelia said encouragingly.

"I really don't know," Pam said, her mood growing darker again. Either the police had the evidence or they didn't, she said. "There's nothing I can do to stop what is going to happen."

Cecelia suggested that her best course of action might be to confess that she and Bill had an affair but that she did not kill Gregg.

"Well, I'm not going to do that now," Pam replied. "I'm not going to say that he stayed over at my house. I'm just going to say that I went out with him or something. And then I went over to his house and fucked him? I'm not going to say that."

Pam glanced at her watch. It was almost time for her appointment with her psychiatrist, another indication that the stress was getting to her.

"Remember what I told you," she repeated to Cecelia. "The police will try and be your fucking best friend, and then they'll turn right against you and they'll fucking say, 'Okay, we want to explain to you what harboring a crime is, and if you'll do this and do that,' well, you'll go, 'Oh, okay.' Great. Then they'll say you have the fucking right to remain silent."

Cecelia admitted she was still worried about the specter of a lie detector test.

Pam brushed it off. "Tell them, 'I'm fucking fifteen years old. I'm fucking nervous. What the hell, man, all my friends are arrested for murder. . . .' You know."

Before leaving, Pam reiterated "don't forget about the accessory angle. . . . If you confess, you're going to have more problems than you ever had. You know right now your problems are just inside you, like the way you feel about everything and how you wish you fucking didn't know anything. There's nothing you can do about that. But if you think people bother you now with questions, you know it's never going to fucking end. I mean, just let it end with the fact that you don't know anything."

13

IN EACH SUCCEEDING CONVERSATION between Pam and Cecelia, Pam got bolder in her admissions. In the first two telephone conversations, she danced all around the subject of Gregg's murder without committing herself. In the July 12 conversation in her office, she was much more explicit, virtually confessing that she set up the killing and not denying it when Cecelia said as much. At the July 12 meeting, she also strongly hinted that Cecelia should either be willing to lie about what she knew or keep her mouth shut.

On July 13—the dreaded Friday the 13th—in a conversation that took place in the parking lot outside her office, Pam made her position irrevocably clear. The time, as it had been the day before, was at the shag end of the lunch hour. When Pam drove up, she found Cecelia waiting for her. The first question she asked was about Cecelia's scheduled meeting with the investigator from the attorney general's office.

"I didn't go," Cecelia said. "Captain Jackson [of the Derry police] called, and he wants to meet with me at three-thirty. I'm not going to the attorney general's today."

That was just as well, Pam said, because the legal proceedings were beginning to steamroll. Her lawyers had told her that a grand jury was looking into the matter.

"They're going to subpoena me, Pam," Cecelia said worriedly. "I know they are."

"They are," Pam agreed. "They're going to subpoena everyone, any friends I have."

"What happens if I lie on the stand and they find out?" Cecelia asked.

"How would they find out?"

"I mean, if somebody says that I did know?"

"Who would know? Who would say that?"

"Does J.R. know what I know?"

"Even if he did know that," Pam said reassuringly, "it's his word against yours, and they can't prove it."

"I mean, obviously I knew about [Gregg's murder] beforehand, and if I get up there and lie, and then if they find out about it, I'm going to get in trouble."

"Well, if you didn't know about it beforehand and you say you knew about it beforehand, you're going to be in trouble [too]."

"Well, I did know about it beforehand," Cecelia insisted.

"Yeah, but if you say that, you're going to get in trouble anyway. So you're better off just lying.

[To convict you] they would have to have evidence that you knew. Somebody saying something like that is hearsay. Like [Bill, Pete, and J.R.] are never going to get convicted for murder unless they have fingerprints and hair and shit, you know what I mean? Like they're never just going to get convicted because [of what] Ralph said. They're not, you know, and right now they could give two flying shits about anything regarding anybody else."

As before, Pam seemed more worried about her affair with Bill being exposed than about being tied to her husband's murder. As she had in the conversation the previous day, she expressed concern that police may have found a note Bill had written her expressing his devotion. Cecelia, on the other hand, was focused on the murder.

"What did they do with the stuff they stole [from the condo]?" she asked.

"I don't know," Pam replied. "I have no idea."

"Did they really steal stuff?"

"Yeah," said Pam. "Things were stolen from my house, but I don't know [what happened to them]. I would assume they threw it out.

"I should hope so," Cecelia added. "I hope it isn't lying in Bill's bedroom or something."

Pam laughed. "I don't know," she said, "but I doubt it. I highly doubt it."

Despite Cecelia's attempts to get Pam to talk

about the time when Bill was supposed to have killed Gregg in April and deliberately got lost, Pam wouldn't bite.

"It's history now," she said. "We can't talk about shit that should have happened."

As if that reminded her, Pam brought up her telephone conversation with Cecelia of a month before, the one that had been taped by officers.

"I don't know if my phone's been tapped," she said, "but if it was, there was a time when I was talking to you on the phone and you said to me, 'You should have just got divorced.' Something like that. Hopefully, my phone wasn't tapped because I could have shit when you said that."

What investigators were really looking for, Pam explained pointedly, was someone who knew about the events before they occurred. "Then they can really bag them, you know."

To make sure she was getting her point across, she made it even clearer.

"I hate the fact that you have to be interviewed," she said. "I hate the fact that you're scared. I hate the fact that you're probably going to have to take a lie detector test. But I don't know what to tell you. If I thought if you told the truth it was going to do you any good, that's one thing. But it's not. You cannot change what you know, you know. You can't. And if you tell the fucking truth, you are probably going to be arrested. And even if you're not arrested, you're going to have to send Bill, you're going to have to send Pete, you're going to have to send J.R., and you're going to have to send me to the fucking slammer for the rest of our entire lives. Unfortunately, that's the situation you're in."

Pausing for breath, she continued: "I think your parents will get over the fact that you decided you didn't want to take a lie detector test, but I don't think they will get over the fact that for the next two years you're going to be going to trial sending everybody up."

As if a new thought suddenly occurred to her, Pam stared at Cecelia. Laughing mirthlessly, she said: "I feel like totally feeling you because I'm afraid one day you're going to come in here and you're going to be wired by the fucking police and I'm going to be busted."

Cecelia didn't know what to say, so she said the first thing that popped into her head. "All I can say is, if Raymond hadn't have run his mouth off . . ."

Pam continued staring at her. "Give me some signal," she said, "if you ever come down to me and you're wired."

Praying that her relief at escaping a body search wasn't too apparent, Cecelia mumbled, "I'll wink.

"All I have to say is," she continued, "if Raymond hadn't run his frigging mouth off, this would have been the perfect murder—"

"Right."

"—because they set everything up—"

"No shit."

"—to look like a burglary just like you said."

"No shit. So it's not my fault. Fucking Raymond—"

"Had not run his mouth off, everything was set up perfect."

"No shit," Pam said. "But the thing you have to realize is that no matter what, Bill's not going to drag you into it. What good would that do? Plus, Pete and J.R. never talked to you about the murder, right? They never said, 'Oh, Cecelia, you know!' Right?"

"No," conceded Cecelia.

"So as far as they know, Bill [only] told them you knew. That doesn't really mean you knew, you know. It's just going to be their word, their convicted-criminal-arrested-for-murder word against yours."

"Yeah," Cecelia agreed.

"So you have to go there and just fucking say the same goddamn fucking story and don't change it. And that's it."

Certain that things were going to get a lot worse before they got better, Pam tried to prepare Cecelia for what might be coming.

"All I know is that pretty soon J.R. is going to roll [over and confess]," Pam said. "He was supposedly only in the car. I don't know. I have no idea. [But] pretty soon he is going to be, like, 'Fuck Pete and Bill; I'm not going to jail for the rest of my goddamn fucking life.' So he is going to turn against them, and he is going to blame me.

"I *know* he is," she continued. "And that's when I am going to be in trouble. That's when I am going to get arrested."

Unexpectedly she turned optimistic. "But I can probably get out of it," she said, "because they are not going to have any proof. I never said any words like 'J.R., I will pay you to kill Gregg.' I never said anything. J.R. never talked to me about the murder or anything. Bill could have told them all that I would pay them. I don't know what Bill told them to get them to go. [But] they're not going to have any proof. They can't convict me because of fucking J.R.'s sixteen-year-old-word-in-the-slammer-facing-the-rest-of-his-life."

Cecelia decided to take the role of devil's advocate. "Well, first of all," she said, "you didn't offer to pay him, right?"

"No," said Pam, meaning that was correct, that she did not offer to pay him.

"So he's not going to say you offered to pay him. He's going to say you knew about it before it happened, which is the truth."

"Right," said Pam. "So then I'll have to say, 'No, I didn't,' and then they're going to believe me or they are going to believe J.R.-sixteen-years-old-in-the-slammer. And then [who will they believe]? Me, with a professional reputation! That's the thing. They are going to believe me."

Cecelia looked skeptical. "All right," she said. "Well, I'll call you."

Pam invited her to come over that evening so they would go out. "You'd better be there," she added laughingly, "or I'll come after you with my Rambo knife."

Ironically Pam did not know at the time how correctly she had predicted events. Cecelia *was* wired, just as she feared. And Cecelia *would* later testify against her, as would Bill, Pete, and J.R.

A big flaw in Pam's reasoning revolved around the issue of credibility. Although it was true that she was a professional with a sterling reputation throughout high school and college, while her opponents were unformed adolescents from the wrong side of the tracks, she failed to anticipate how dramatic their testimony would be.

She also did not recognize how cold and uncaring she would appear when she was thrown into the public eye. Perhaps in her view it was the duty of a successful TV anchorperson to remain detached no matter what was going on, but that obviously did not apply when a person's own life was at stake. Not for nothing would she be dubbed the "Ice Princess."

The error of her obsession with keeping her affair with Bill secret, even over defending herself against accusations of setting up the murder of her husband, apparently would not dawn on Pam until it was too late.

But the fourth and perhaps most serious oversight on her part was just how incriminating her conversations with Cecelia were. That also would not be brought home for several months, but when it was made clear the effects would be devastating.

For her part, Cecelia had been correct about one major issue as well. When Pam kept insisting that she was safe because she had never offered money to Bill, Pete or J.R., Cecelia had correctly envisioned that the more serious issue was not money, but the fact that she knew in advance about the murder.

On August 1, just a little more than two weeks after the July 13 conversation with Cecelia, Pam was arrested.

14

NEW HAMPSHIRE NEWSAHOLICS had a field day in August; the media attention given to Pam's arrest overshadowed even that devoted to the capture of J.R., Bill, and Pete. What made it even better from one point of view was the knowledge that her arrest was just the beginning: Young widow picked up; salacious details to come. And come they would, but at the beginning the story was treated circumspectly, considering the circumstances.

The *Union Leader* gave the story top play on August 2: the entire top fourth of the front page. Under a headline reading POLICE SAY WIDOW HELPED TEEN MURDER HER HUSBAND, writer Cissy Taylor went straight to the point: "Pamela A. Smart was arrested yesterday and charged as an accomplice in the murder of her husband, Gregory, whom prosecutors said she wanted dead because she was in love with someone else."

After a promising start, however, the story fizzled out because most of the juicy details were still being kept under wraps by law enforcement officials. Complicating the problem was the fact that Bill, J.R., and Pete were still being legally treated as juveniles, as in truth they were. The state attorney general's office was working to have them certified as adults, but until that could be accomplished their names could not be revealed and some of the particulars about the crime were held back. Although police formally turned over some documentation (only as much as was felt necessary to make sure Pam stayed in jail), large sections were blacked out by a judge in Derry, including the teens' names. Bill, for example, was referred to in the documents as "William F.," while J.R. and Pete were not identified at all.

The *Telegraph* gave similar prominence to the story, but it had more details. It mentioned, for instance, some of the events that occurred before the teens' arrests, such as Vance Lattime, Sr., whom it did not mention by name, taking the pistol to police. The *Telegraph*'s Diane Rietman also noted—sans names—how J.R. waited at Hood Plaza; how Bill had spent at least some time at Pam's condo in Derry; how Pam gave last-minute instructions to the teens; how Gregg had two life insurance policies with Pam as beneficiary; and how Ralph blew the whistle. The story also alluded to other incidents that would not be revealed in detail until later, such as Cecelia overhearing Pam and Gregg arguing about divorce and how Pam later said she was going to have to have him killed or she would lose everything.

Just before noon on the day she was arrested, Pam telephoned Judith Smart, her former mother-in-law, to see if she could get information about what investigators were doing in the case. She found out firsthand very quickly. Two hours later, at 1:45 P.M., officers knocked on the door of her office and presented her with a warrant accusing her of being an accomplice to murder, which under New Hampshire law carries a mandatory sentence of life without parole upon conviction. It was nineteen days almost to the minute after her last tape-recorded conversation with Cecelia. Why it took authorities so long to pick her up has never been explained.

Surprisingly, considering the animosity that would soon erupt between the Smarts and Pam, Gregg's younger brother, Rick, publicly came to her defense. "You have to understand," he told reporters, "they dated for three years before they got married. Gregg was smart enough to know who he was marrying. If Gregg could see her in jail now, he'd be shocked and outraged." Rick, however, lived in Nashua, not Derry, and his contact with Pam over the months of his brother's marriage and, particularly, after his murder had been limited.

William Smart, Gregg's father, was by no means in Pam's camp, even at that early stage.

"She has taken a loved one from us," he said at an impromptu news conference in Derry. "If indeed she is guilty, they should teach her a lesson. She should get the maximum sentence that Lord and God above us would give her."

Pam's parents, John and Linda Wojas, declined to talk to reporters.

Their daughter, however, in what had become her customary fashion, showed no such restraint. She had no sooner been locked up than she called the media to make a statement. "People are treating me like I'm the big link between the kids and Gregg's murder," she said sarcastically, questioning the reasoning in ordering the warrant for her arrest.

Immediately she began making efforts to be released. Her attorneys, Paul Twomey and Mark Sisti of Chichester, a tiny community near Concord, asked for a bail hearing as soon as possible in superior court in Exeter, the county seat for Rockingham County. Judge Douglas Gray agreed to hear the petition on Monday, August 13.

During the hearing, Pam, dressed in a black patterned coat and a black skirt, part of her extensive wardrobe of fashionable business clothes, asked to speak in her own behalf.

"I am twenty-two years old," she began disingenuously, since she would celebrate her twenty-third birthday in three days, "and I am a widow. Three months ago my husband was viciously murdered. Since then, I've been wrongly accused of this heinous crime. It's been twelve days that I've been in jail for a crime I did not commit. I have gone through immeasurable pain and suffering. I ask that I can prove my innocence. I can assure you I am not going anywhere. I want to be in this courtroom to prove I am innocent of these charges."

Although Pam's parents had agreed to put up as much as $100,000 as bail (which was how much equity they had built on their house in Canobie Lake), Judge Gray—once he had listened privately to selections from the tape-recorded conversations between Pam and Cecelia—flatly rejected the request. She would have to stay at the Women's State Prison in Goffstown, Gray said, pending new developments in the case.

Some of those developments were not long in coming. The next day a Rockingham County grand jury indicted Pam not only on the accomplice to murder charge, but on two additional charges as well: conspiracy to commit murder and witness tampering. The latter charge stemmed from Pam's attempts to convince Cecelia either not to say anything to authorities or to lie.

The indictment sealed Pam's fate as far as being released on bail was concerned, at least for the immediate future. With the additional charges—conspiracy to commit murder and witness tampering—there was no hope that the court would let her go free until the trial.

* * *

This position was made even clearer several months later. On January 4, 1991, a grand jury in Hillsborough County (the site of the women's prison) indicted Pam on yet three more charges: criminal solicitation of murder; witness tampering (which was a charge distinct from the one for which she was indicted in Rockingham County); and criminal solicitation involving witness tampering.

According to the indictments, Pam had created a rather convoluted plot involving a fellow inmate from D tier named Marianne Moses. If the allegations were to be believed, Pam was going to ask Moses's son George, who was roughly the same age as Bill et al, to testify that he had overheard Cecelia say she had lied about Pam's involvement in Gregg's murder. If that did not work, Pam wanted Moses, who was serving two to four years for welfare fraud, to locate, through her husband, an assassin to kill Cecelia.

Pam's attorneys angrily labeled the new charges "garbage" and said they were concocted by only one of a number of inmates who had "lined up" to say derogatory things about Pam so they could have a brief moment in the spotlight.

Later, the judge at Pam's Rockingham County trial would rule that Moses would not be allowed to testify about the alleged plot until she provided the defense with the telephone number she supposedly used to reach her husband when she called him about a possible assassin. The woman refused to divulge the information, saying her husband was wanted for allegedly robbing a bank and if she turned over what the defense wanted, he could be traced and arrested.

Eventually the attorney general's office dismissed the Hillsborough County charges, but at the time they were a very live issue.

It was yet another irony in the case that the charges alleged the possible assassination of Cecelia Pierce. In the tapes of Pam's conversations with Cecelia, Pam had specifically told Cecelia not to worry, despite the reports that Pam, armed with a "Rambo knife," had come looking for her. She would never do anything to try to harm her, Pam promised. Yet six months later she was accused of shopping for someone to do her in.

As it turned out, the indictments simply kicked off what would be a major spurt of activity that month relating to the Pam Smart case.

On January 28 Raymond Fowler, the fourth teenager allegedly involved in Gregg's death, was arrested and charged with attempted murder and conspiracy to commit murder.

On that same day, Bill, Pete, and J.R. formalized a plea-bargaining agreement their lawyers had been working out with the attorney general's office. The three of them pleaded guilty in Rockingham County Superior Court as adults.

Bill pleaded to a reduced charge of second-degree murder for killing Gregg, while Pete and J.R. pleaded to reduced charges of accomplices to second-degree murder. In return for their pleas, they would receive less severe sentences.

Under the agreements, Bill and Pete would accept sentences of forty years in prison with twelve years deferred for good behavior. Since the degree of J.R.'s participation was judged to be somewhat less, he would be sentenced to thirty years with twelve years deferred. What that meant was that if Bill and Pete each behaved himself in prison, that is if neither tried to escape or became a major troublemaker, each could be out in twenty-eight years. Pete was only three months older than Bill. At the end of the twenty-eight-year sentence each would be forty-five years old. J.R., on the other hand, a year older than the others, was looking at only eighteen years in prison and could possibly be freed at age thirty-six.

Because the three pleaded guilty, they would not be tried. But there was one more condition in the plea-bargain agreement that they would have to keep before they could relax: each of them promised to testify against Pam.

15

WHILE THE FOCUS, of course, would remain on Pamela Smart and her alleged involvement in the death of her husband, what helped make it such a riveting case for the public was the fact that the murder allegedly involved teenagers, one of whom was having a sexual affair with a school official, a professional woman half a dozen years his senior.

The perception that Pam was a teacher continued to persist, even though she was not. And that would call attention to the phenomenon of sexual relationships between students and teachers or other school officials.

It is, perhaps, a sign of the times that sooner or later some attention would be given to sexual liaisons between teachers and students when the teacher is a female and her student partner is a male. In the past, public attention usually went to cases in which the sexual roles were reversed.

However, after Pam's arrest, there was considerable discussion of this little publicized situation. After August 1990 news media began reporting a number of such incidents.

There was, for instance, a case in New Mexico in which a nurse's aide at a middle school called in sick for a male student so he could drive her van to Santa Fe. Upon investigation it was learned that the relationship apparently went much further. Allegedly she was having sex with that student and one other on a regular basis, plus she was using her house as a party site for students from the school.

Closer to home, in Pam's case, was a situation in Massachusetts, in which a thirty-three-year-old female special-education teacher (who, like Pam, was married) was accused of having sexual relations with a fifteen-year-old male student several times during 1990, once on Valentine's Day, the day before Pam seduced Bill. In that case the older woman was an actual teacher, however, as opposed to the situation that existed with Pam. The woman has denied the charges.

Education officials say the incidences of teacher/student sex, even when the teacher is a female, are more common than most people realize. One educator, Victor Ross of Aurora, Colorado, wrote a book about the subject entitled *The Forbidden Apple*.

Although such liaisons are arguably immoral, not all are illegal. A lot depends on the age of the student. Different states have different laws, with some setting the age of minority at earlier periods, although sixteen seems to be the normal cutoff date. Complicating the issue, however, is the existence of a professional relationship between the people involved.

In other words, if the older person is in a position of authority over the younger one, such as teacher/student, the legal age of the younger one usually rises. If sixteen is the age at which a person can legally have sex with someone else in a particular state, for example, the age might well be eighteen if the older partner is in a position of authority over the younger one.

In New Hampshire, if a sixteen-year-old student agrees to have sex with a teacher or other school official—absent any attempt at coercion—it is not against the law. But it does not have to be illegal for repercussions to kick in. In New Hampshire if a *teacher* has sex with a sixteen-year-old (or older) student, the teacher can be fired and lose certification.

Pam undoubtedly feared she would be fired if her affair with Bill was known, teacher or not. From all indications she really enjoyed her job, and that may have been why she was so paranoid, which was evident in her conversations with Cecelia, about the story of the affair leaking out.

Following Pam's arrest, New Hampshire authorities confirmed that within the previous eighteen months three teachers in the state had their teaching certificates revoked because they either attempted to seduce a student or had an affair.

Sometimes criminal charges are involved. For instance, a twenty-one-year-old substance-abuse adviser (again, *not* a teacher) in New Hampshire was charged not long after Pam was arrested with raping a sixteen-year-old girl he was counseling.

But sometimes nothing at all happens, legally speaking. In another New Hampshire case a female teacher in her mid-twenties was discovered to be having an affair with one of the students in her school. The student was a junior, which put him over the age of sixteen. However, the affair had been going on since the student was in the ninth grade, when he was younger than sixteen. The liaison was discovered when the teacher announced that she was pregnant and subsequently resigned. She and the student went to another state to get married.

A number of cases of teacher/student relationships go completely unnoticed, either because they flare up and die down too quickly or because the participants are able to keep their secrets. Also, in virtually every educational jurisdiction, there is no system set up to keep statistics on such incidents, which makes it extremely difficult to say with any certainty how prevalent such situations are.

The fact that such situations occur, however, should not be surprising. The teenage years are times of sexual blossoming. That is the time when teenagers want to try out their newfound sexual powers, not only on their peers, but on adults with whom they come in regular contact, such as teachers. On the other hand, some adults can be especially attracted to teenagers, especially when the teenagers are physically mature.

Psychological maturity plays an important role in such relationships as well, and there was considerable debate during Pam's trial about whether Pam was not on the same maturity level as Bill, with the implication being that she was less mature than would have been expected for a woman her age. In other words, even if the physical attraction was there, she should have known better.

Although Pam mentioned almost casually to Cecelia that she was seeing a psychiatrist, there was never, unfortunately, any psychological testimony introduced at her trial, so there was no guideline to go by when trying to assign psychological motivation to the events that transpired.

Pam's case also brought to the forefront another American phenomenon that is gaining increasing attention: females who kill.

Throughout history there has never been a paucity of villainesses, but of late, it seems, there has been an inordinate number in our society. Just within a few months in the same time frame as Pam's case, for example, there have been half a dozen juicy cases.

Take Carolyn Warmus, for example, who, interestingly enough, was a schoolteacher. Since she taught the fifth grade, however, she was not sexually involved with one of her students. But she *was* involved with a married man. The prosecutor in White Plains, New York, contended that Warmus killed the man's wife, shooting her nine times and leaving her lying in a pool of blood, so she could have her lover full-time. On April 27, 1991, the judge in the case declared a mistrial after jurors said they were unable to agree on a verdict. The group was hung up with eight jurors voting for conviction and four against. The district attorney's office said it would seek a new trial.

In Detroit a young woman named Toni Cato Riggs is awaiting trial on charges of masterminding the killing of her soldier husband, who had just returned from the Gulf, for his insurance money.

In Wisconsin there is the ongoing saga of Lawrencia "Bambi" Bembenek, who was convicted of killing her husband's ex-wife. But she resurfaced in the headlines last summer when she escaped. She was recaptured in Canada.

In Washington, Pennsylvania, near Pittsburgh, a twenty-nine-year-old woman named Mary Kay Cassidy also is awaiting trial on charges of murdering her husband. Allegedly she was taped plotting the homicide.

In Dallas there was the case of Joy Aylor, a well-known and socially prominent interior decorator who allegedly hired one or more hit men to kill her estranged husband's mistress and then try to kill him, even though by that time he was her ex-husband. Aylor was arrested in the spring of 1991 in France, where she had been living under an assumed name. She remains incarcerated in France. Texas authorities are seeking to extradite her to stand trial on charges of murder and solicitation of murder. The Dallas District Attorney's office wants to seek the death penalty against Aylor, but French officials have indicated they will not extradite her if there is a possibility she may be executed.

Perhaps hiring assassins has become a new fad in Texas because another Texan, Wanda Holloway of suburban Houston, is also awaiting trial on charges of trying to hire a hit man. Instead of her husband, Holloway allegedly tried to hire someone to kill a neighbor. The supposed reason: The woman's daughter was competing with Holloway's daughter for a much-sought-after slot on the junior high school cheerleading squad.

Whatever has spurred this public interest, the fact that it exists is undeniable. When Pam went on trial in the Rockingham County Courthouse in Exeter, the ensuing mob scene was described by more than one participant as a "circus." This characterization was not far off.

More than one hundred reporters wanted to attend the trial, including one from Israel and several from the United Kingdom, not to mention hundreds of area residents. Since the number of courtroom seats was limited, court officials had to devise a plan that would allow as many people as possible inside and still maintain a position of fairness. What they did was set aside three rows of seats for the media, plus another row each for the families of Pam and Gregg. The remaining seats—about thirty—went to the public on a first-come first-served basis. As a result, would-be trial watchers began lining up long before the courthouse doors opened to get a ticket assuring them a seat. As the trial progressed and the testimony grew increasingly salacious, the number of people who wanted to attend also increased. So they started queuing earlier. By the time Pam was ready to testify, people were lining up shortly after midnight, in the middle of a New England winter, in hopes of getting one of the prized tickets.

Naturally not everyone was accommodated. But to make it less disappointing for those who wanted to be close to the action, the overflow of people who could not get into the courtroom itself was shuttled into two anterooms where they could view the proceedings on TV.

Also, the state's leading television station, WMUR, an ABC affiliate, decided early on to broadcast the trial live, preempting even the popular middle-of-the-day soap operas.

This had been a difficult decision to make since the time period for the trial not only overlapped with the soaps, but also coincided with the climax of the Gulf War, which had been drawing a record-setting TV viewership. But in the end the decision proved to be a wise move for the Manchester station, the one where Pam had once applied for a job as a newswoman. The trial drew more viewers than any other program broadcast by the station since it went on the air in 1954. When Cecelia's tapes were played in the courtroom, WMUR estimated that 84,000 households were tuned in. And that was the middle of the day. When those who had been at work returned home and switched on the evening news, 114,000 homes were glued to WMUR.

In addition to the crowds normally attracted to such events, Pam's trial also drew its share of publicity seekers, like the forty-year-old man who said he was working on a degree in elementary education at a small upstate college. Daily he paraded in front of the courthouse with a sign proclaiming "In America you are innocent until proven guilty. Pame is innocent [until proven guilty]."

Pame claimed to be innocent, too.

16

As THE SEASONS CHANGED from summer to fall to winter, and 1990 gave way to 1991, the elements necessary for the trial of Pam Smart clicked resolutely into place. By January the main players—that is, the ones who would have major roles in the big production—were all in position.

Presiding would be fifty-seven-year-old Douglas Roberts Gray, who looked exactly like the popular conception of a New Englander. Long, tall, taciturn, with a wit as dry as a Baptist banquet, Gray was definitely Jimmy Stewartish, although he later confessed that he thought of himself as more like Clint Eastwood.

A superior court judge since 1983, when he was lured out of private practice in the town of Rye and named to the bench by then Governor John Sununu, Gray was not one to try to duck a controversial case. His first big media exposure came in 1987 in a case involving a man named Mark Murabito and his former wife, Jesse.

It started out as an unexceptional divorce and custody fight until Jesse accused her former husband of sexually abusing the two kids. After listening to testimony during the divorce proceeding, Gray ruled that the children had *not* been abused and he later granted Mark visiting rights.

Jesse persisted in the abuse accusations, however, and Mark subsequently was indicted for sexually assaulting his five-year-old daughter. Gray also presided at Mark's criminal trial, during which Mark was acquitted.

When the verdict came in, Jesse took the children and fled, eventually ending up in the tiny Montana town of Loma, where she was discovered and brought back to New Hampshire.

For his actions, Gray caught flak from both sides. In the end, at Jesse's request, Gray removed himself from any other proceedings involving the couple and their children. But in 1990 another judge substantiated Gray's ruling by granting Mark sole custody.

And in 1990 he presided at two trials of a man named George Gurney, Jr., who was accused of kidnapping his former wife, shooting her and leaving her for dead, and then murdering her lover with a gun, a knife, and his fists. Both trials ended in hung juries. Gray was forced to free Gurney when the attorney general's office decided to dismiss the charges rather than go through a third trial.

But never had Gray been party to a case that would get the publicity afforded Pam's trial.

The controversy in Pam's case began almost immediately when Gray refused a defense request for a change of venue. Pam, through her attorneys, had claimed that she could not receive a fair trial in Rockingham County because of the large amount of publicity that had been given to her case, most of which she claimed was prejudiced against her. To back up their argument, Mark Sisti and Paul Twomey pointed out that the case had been covered exhaustively by the media in both New Hampshire and Boston and had appeared on a number of syndicated television programs such as "Inside Edition," "Hard Copy," "Sally Jesse Raphael," "Geraldo," "Oprah," and "Donahue."

Gray's decision to refuse to grant the change of venue motion could come back to haunt him. Sisti and Twomey later said it might be an issue if they decide to appeal.

In her July 12 conversation with Cecelia, Pam had said that her lawyers were the best anywhere. Even factoring in a certain amount of hyperbole, they certainly were reputed to be good.

Mark Sisti, thirty-six, and Paul Twomey, forty-one, were working as public defenders when they decided to team up four years ago. Sisti, who grew up in Buffalo, New York, and went to law school at Franklin Pierce in Concord, is the more aggressive of the two. Because of this, it was decided that he would handle the cross-examination during Pam's trial. A pudgy, jolly-looking fellow with a high forehead and a roundish face, Sisti became know to thousands of TV watchers as a balding man (because the camera was focused almost continuously on his back) with a combative approach to questioning designed to throw an unwary witness off his stride.

Twomey, a native of Worcester, Massachusetts, and a graduate of the University of Wisconsin, is so soft-spoken that at times he was almost unintelligible over the occasionally balky courtroom sound system. A special-education teacher who went into the law late, Twomey's forte was providing a soothing presence for defense witnesses. A tall, thin man with a wide mouth, narrow face, and a droopy forelock, Twomey handled the summation after all the evidence was presented, while Sisti delivered the opening statement.

On the other side were two young prosecutors from the attorney general's office, Paul Maggiotto and Diane M. Nicolosi. In New Hampshire, the attorney general's office has criminal as well as civil jurisdiction. Although counties also have prosecutors, it is assistant attorneys general who take on homicides. It is an indicator of either the relatively small size of the state (one million people) or the efficiency of the attorney general's office (no acquittals in a homicide case since 1988) or the relative absence of serious crime in the state—or all of the preceding—that all of New Hampshire's murderers can be prosecuted by fewer than a dozen assistants in the criminal bureau.

Maggiotto, a wiry, intense man with thick curly black hair, would be the lead counsel, and Nicolosi would be the backup. What that meant in practical terms was that Maggiotto would examine the main witnesses, like Bill and Pam, and would deliver the summation of the prosecution's case. Nicolosi, on the other hand, would present the opening statement and examine the other witnesses.

Nicolosi, a slim, poised woman with wavy light-brown hair tumbling to her shoulders, grew up in Methuen, Massachusetts, but went to the University of New Hampshire for her undergraduate degree. She attended law school at the Franklin Pierce Law Center in Concord and clerked for a year in superior court after she graduated in 1986. After that she worked in the AG's transportation and construction bureau, handling civil litigation, before transferring to the criminal bureau. When she was assigned to Pam's case she already had two homicide trials behind her. She celebrated her thirty-second birthday the day after Bill, Pete, and J.R. accepted their plea-bargain arrangements, less than three weeks before jury selection began.

Maggiotto, an easily identifiable New Yorker, grew up in the city, although he went to law school in Boston. After graduating from Northeastern University he signed on with the district attorney's office in Brooklyn and spent five and a half years prosecuting sex crime violators and murderers. During his time in Brooklyn, Maggiotto tried some two dozen major felony cases, about half of them homicides.

In 1989 he and his wife, also a prosecutor, decided to start a family. But that decision led to another: Did they want to raise their children in the city? The answer was no; there was too much crime. So they started looking around for a place to relocate, somewhere quieter, more peaceful, and less dangerous.

At the recommendation of a friend, Maggiotto sent a résumé to the New Hampshire Attorney General's Office. In a move that surprised him, he was invited for an interview. One thing led to another, and on April 1, 1990—April Fool's Day, he joked later—he and his wife started working in almost identical offices in Concord across Capitol Street from the statehouse.

It was still another irony of the Pam Smart case that two of the major players had come to New Hampshire fleeing crime: John Wojas had run away from Miami, and Paul Maggiotto had decamped from New York City. In an Exeter courtroom these men with strikingly similar goals were to find themselves deeply involved in the worst of all possible crimes, homicide, and its aftermath. But they would be on opposite sides; Maggiotto would be trying to send Wojas's daughter to prison for the rest of her life.

Jury selection began on Tuesday, February 19. A week later the process was completed. From the list of registered voters in Rockingham County, prosecution and defense attorneys had agreed to a panel of eight men and seven women, which included three alternates. When the alternates were weeded out after the trial, the decision on Pam's guilt would be made by seven women and five men, a diverse group whose members included a software engineer, a retired banker, a seventy-five-year-old widow, and a graduate student. The foreperson was a middle-aged nurse.

In the prosecution's opening statement, Nicolosi argued that Pam cold-bloodedly manipulated Bill, using threats to withhold sex and affection, into killing Gregg because she didn't want to go through the hassle of a divorce and risk losing her furniture and her dog. "It was that woman," Nicolosi said, pointing dramatically at Pam, "who initiated, orchestrated, and directed the killing."

Speaking for the defense, Sisti contended that Bill, Pete, and J.R. plotted the murder on their own, *without Pam's knowledge*, because Bill was obsessed with Pam and was jealous of Gregg. He said Pam repeatedly tried to break off the affair, but Bill refused to comply. The others joined their friend, Sisti claimed, because they were "young thrill killers." After they were caught, he added, they conspired to frame Pam so they could escape sentences of life without parole.

The drama would be played out in a solid-looking brick-and-concrete building on the edge of Exeter, a facility outfitted with a metal detector at the door and a bomb-sniffing dog named Brutus inside—just in case.

The proceedings formally began on Tuesday, March 5, one day after the jury went on an escorted bus tour of the murder site in Derry and of Pam's office in Hampton, and two days after Gray ruled that J.R., Pete, and Bill would be allowed to testify despite defense objections. The first major witness was Patrick "Pete" Randall.

17

JUDGE GRAY'S COURTROOM was a cozy sort of place, with adequate but unostentatious lighting and walls paneled in warm oak. It was so cozy, in fact, that the defense and prosecution shared the same side of the room.

Commonly, the defense table and the prosecution table sit facing the bench from opposite sides of a center aisle, which usually assumes the aspect of a deep canyon. In Rockingham County, however, the adversaries were virtually on top of each other.

Both attorneys' tables were on the left side of the room (the judge's right), with the prosecution's being the closest to the bench. Directly behind the prosecution table, only a few feet away, was the defense table. The disadvantage in such a situation, for the prosecution, was that in order to observe Pam's reaction to testimony, Maggiotto or Nicolosi had to turn completely around. Or if Nicolosi and Maggiotto wanted to confer, Twomey or Sisti were staring straight at the backs of their necks. If this arrangement made any of them uncomfortable, however, it was not evident.

When questioning a witness, the lawyers used a lectern set up in front of the jury box, which was on the other side of the room. In some courtrooms, lawyers pace and wave their arms and engage in all sorts of histrionics, but not in New Hampshire, at least not in Judge Gray's court.

Part of the reason for this, however, was that the television camera was in the rear of the room behind the lectern, so the witness was facing directly into it and the examining lawyer exposed his bald spot. The camera could swivel to the left, to take in the prosecution and defense tables and even part of the spectator section, but it could not swivel to the right to the jury box. The jury was never shown.

Some judges play a very vocal role during a trial, making comments, chattering with the attorneys, or asking questions. Gray was not a vocal judge. Except for a ruling on an occasional objection, he said so little that it was easy to forget he was there.

By the same token, Maggiotto and Nicolosi were not flashy prosecutors, and they worked through their first few witnesses—one of Pam's former neighbors and a handful of police officers—quickly and adeptly, clearing the way for the midafternoon appearance of the first of their stars: Pete.

* * *

Clad in a maroon crew-neck sweater and projecting the personality of a floor lamp, Pete related in a grating monotone the events leading up to Gregg's murder. His dispassion made the event seem remote, rather like a bad novel being read aloud by an eighth-grader, but after a few minutes the gravity of his tale began to sink in and there was not a sound in the courtroom other than his flat voice.

A clean-cut youth with long dark hair parted down the middle, he showed no remorse as he told how he and Bill had waited in the Smarts' condo for Gregg to return and how he had still been holding Gregg's head when Bill pumped a bullet into his brain. He had not cut Gregg's throat as planned, he explained, to do, was because of the brief exchange he had with Gregg about his wedding ring. When he said that Gregg refused to give it to him because his "wife would kill him," Pete said he "freaked out."

"Were you touched?" Maggiotto asked.

"I wasn't touched," Pete replied. "I was scared."

Either he was well coached or he had an amazing memory for detail, because as he spoke he recalled almost minute by minute things that had no real relevance to the case but provided considerable substance to his testimony.

After they picked up the car from J.R.'s grandmother and were heading back to Seabrook to get Rayme, Pete recounted how they had stopped for gas . . . how, while they were waiting in Derry for it to get dark, he had popped into a pizza place to use the restroom . . . how Bill wore a black sweat suit while his was gray . . . how he had first grabbed a pillowcase off the bed to use as a loot bag but had swapped it for a black one because he didn't like the pattern of tiny flowers on a baby blue background . . . how he and Bill had discussed throwing a towel over Gregg's head when he opened the door and then had discarded both the idea and the towel. One got the impression that if Maggiotto had asked how much gas they'd put in the car and what the charge was, Pete could have told him.

His recall was just as detailed when he told of the hours immediately before police arrested him, along with J.R. and Bill.

After his confrontation with Ralph Welch, when he realized that Ralph almost certainly was going to go to the police, Pete said he and J.R. went to Pam's condo, which was just across the athletic fields from Winnacunnet High, because they knew that Bill would be there.

In a desperate attempt to save the situation, Bill telephoned Ralph and tried to convince him that what Pete had told him the night before was just a big joke. The attempt was spectacularly unsuccessful. The three youths knew it would only be a matter of time before they were arrested.

After giving his mother a brief explanation of the kind of trouble he was in, Pete borrowed her car and the three made the hour-and-a-half drive to a relative's house in Connecticut, intending to lay low out of state until they could work out a better plan. While there, Pete's father reached him by telephone and told him to bring the car home or he was going to report it stolen.

Dejected, the three returned to Seabrook to wait for the police to come for them.

The end came the next evening, he said. Bored and nervous from sitting around J.R.'s house, the three went to a movie. Halfway through the film, Patricia Randall and Diane Lattime came into the theater to get them. "The police are waiting for you," they told their sons. "It's time to go."

Throughout the entire tale, Pete remained completely matter-of-fact. He may have been an automaton regurgitating whatever had been programmed into him, except it was too graphic, too elaborate, not to be authentic.

Pete's direct testimony ran past quitting time, so he was recalled the next morning. The only change evidenced by the overnight break was that on Wednesday he wore a blue sweater instead of a red one. His tone and demeanor remained unmodified.

Glancing from Pete, who was about as stoical as one could get, to Pam, who sat just as imperturbably at the defense table in a white granny dress and a flowered bow in her long blond hair, one wondered why they disliked each other so much when, at least outwardly, they seemed so much alike.

* * *

On cross-examination, Sisti underlined this dislike that Pete and Pam had for each other, pointing out that Pete actually had very little contact with Pam and that almost everything he knew about Pam's involvement in the murder was filtered through Bill.

"Pame wasn't there on the night of the killing, right? She didn't send an instruction booklet?"

Pete conceded that was correct. But despite obvious efforts to shake him up, Sisti was unable to raise any more emotion in him than Maggiotto had. Neither was he able to prize loose any significantly damaging information.

Thanks to Sisti's persistence, Pete admitted that on the night of the murder he had taken several gold chains out of the jewelry he had stolen from the Smarts to Hampton Beach, where he'd tried to trade them for cocaine.

"You didn't say that yesterday, remember?" prodded Sisti.

"That's correct," Pete mumbled, tucking his chin closer to his chest like a boxer waiting for a punch.

"When we say we're going to Hampton Beach, we're not just going for a stroll, right? You're going so you can blow some coke up your nose, right?"

"I wanted to get my mind off what had happened," Pete replied.

Sisti also got Pete to admit that he had in the past engaged in other illegal activities, such as stealing stereos and radios out of cars, pirating motorcycles, and buying dope. "Occasionally," Pete responded quietly every time Sisti brought up a different illegal enterprise.

The defense attorney obviously was trying to paint Pete as a petty thief in the jury's eyes, a youth who had no qualms about stealing anything that wasn't nailed down. But the purpose of the exercise was dubious: Pete had already pleaded guilty to murder, and one could hardly admit to anything worse than that.

Without much prompting, however, Pete readily admitted he did not find jail a very pleasant place, even though the Rockingham County facility where he was then being kept was more like a dormitory than a prison, with individual rooms whose doors were left open in the daytime so that the inmates could roam freely within the confines. He was in one room, and Bill and J.R. shared another two doors down, so they could easily visit. But that was the only saving grace about the situation.

"You don't want to be in jail very long, do you?" Sisti asked.

"I'd rather not," Pete replied dryly.

"You don't want Bill to go away for very long, do you?"

"I don't want any of us to go to jail for that long."

"How about her?" Sisti asked, pointing at Pam. "You don't care about her."

"I would not like to see her go to jail for that long, either," Pete said.

"Be honest," Sisti pressed, trying to elicit from Pete an admission that he and the others had conspired to frame Pam—were willing to see her go to jail—so they could get lighter sentences. "You don't care about her."

"I don't wish anybody to go to jail," he replied.

On the whole, Sisti was unable to wring a single admission from Pete that contradicted anything he had testified to earlier. Pointing out that he had access to police reports on the murder through his attorneys, Sisti asked if Ralph Welch had been correct when he'd told investigators that Pete had said Raymond was going to have to be killed as well.

"I never talked about killing another person," Pete insisted.

"You never talked about killing Raymond?" Sisti asked in mock disbelief.

"No, I'm positive," Pete said. "If Ralph said that, Ralph is wrong."

Sisti, however, did raise one issue that was never resolved, at least not by Pete.

When police arrived at Pam and Gregg's condo on the night of May 1, they found Gregg's wedding ring on the floor. But Pete insisted he had no idea how it got off Gregg's finger.

"You pried it off, didn't you?" Sisti demanded.

"No, I did not," Pete responded calmly.

"Are you going to look at the jury and tell them you didn't pry the ring off?"

Pete swiveled his head toward the jury box, one of the few times during his several hours of testimony that he had moved anything except his lips. "I didn't pry the ring off."

"Did Bill pry it off?"

"Bill did not pry it off."

"Are you saying that Gregg just took that ring off and threw it on the ground?"

Pete repeated what he had told Maggiotto earlier: when Gregg refused to give him his ring and Pete realized it was a wedding band, he "freaked out."

"Is that what stopped you from slashing his throat?" Sisti asked.

"I just couldn't do it," Pete replied.

18

COMPARED TO PETE, J.R. was a model of animation. Still, he wasn't going to win any Mr. Personality awards.

Leaning slightly over the witness stand, J.R. rambled in a semimonotone, explaining how he and Pete and Bill had been inseparable companions and how they had shared everything. He knew about the sexual relationship between Bill and Pam, he said, because he had seen them kissing in the car in front of his house and because, to while away dull lectures in the crime and punishment class, Bill had showed him love notes that Pam had written.

Even though he knew how close Bill was to Pam, J.R. said, it came as a shock when Bill first mentioned to him that he planned to kill Pam's husband because she had asked him to.

"We thought he was nuts," J.R. said.

Diane Nicolosi asked him what changed his mind, what made him realize that Bill was serious.

"He said that Pam had told him that her and Gregg didn't get along, but if they got a divorce Gregg would get everything. Also, he said Pam had told him that she had been hit by Gregg.

"Did you see any evidence of this bad marriage?" Nicolosi asked.

"I heard one conversation in Pam's office," he related. "Pam switched on the speaker phone, and I heard the end of an argument. I don't know what the argument was about, but it ended, 'Well, if you want a divorce, that's fine by me.' And they both hung up."

"And what conversation did you have with Pamela Smart after that?"

"She said, 'Well, now you see why I have to have this done.'"

He added that although she had not specified what "this" was, he and Bill had already talked about killing Gregg and he understood her to be referring to the plan to murder her husband.

On the afternoon of May 1, he said, corroborating what Pete had said earlier, Pam drove to his house in her CRX with the Halen license plate to pick up the three students and take them to Massachusetts so J.R. could get his grandmother's car. J.R. drove on the way down, he said, because he didn't want to ride in the hatchback area in the back.

On the way down, they reviewed the plans for getting into the condo, with Pam explaining how she had left the bulkhead door open and the back door as well, although Gregg might have come home for lunch and locked it when he left.

"There was a lot of talk about how Pam should act [when she discovered her husband's body], and we all just told her to act normal," J.R. said.

"What was her tone of voice, her emotional state, when she asked how she should react?" Nicolosi asked.

"She seemed a little bit nervous," J.R. replied, "but all of us were."

In response to Nicolosi's question about what else was discussed, J.R. said they talked about how they would kill Gregg.

"Pete said he planned to use a knife. It was quieter and he didn't want to use my father's gun because of ballistics and [because] we couldn't get rid of the gun. My father would have noticed it missing."

Pam, nevertheless, was insistent that a gun be used because of "the mess" a knife would cause "and because she had white leather furniture and stuff."

He paused a second. "At that point she was a little more hysterical," he conceded.

But Bill promised her that he would use the gun, J.R. said, and that calmed her down significantly. "Pete and me didn't say anything," he added.

After they returned to Seabrook and Pam drove off, they went to pick up Raymond Fowler and then stopped at Bill's house so he could get the duffel bag with their change of clothes and the gloves.

"We started making fun of him because of the gloves he had," he said.

"Why was that?" Nicolosi asked.

J.R. shot her an impatient glance. "Because they were latex. If you sweated in them and then put your hand against something like a window, you would leave fingerprints. We were laughing because if he was going to commit a murder, he would need better gloves than that."

They solved the problem, he said, by agreeing to tape their fingertips before they donned the gloves.

After stopping at Bill's house, the drove to Derry and pulled into the parking lot at Hood Plaza. The lot was crowded, he said, because there was some type of activity at the stadium, which was adjacent to the mall. After buying tape for their fingers, he, Bill, and Pete sat in the car waiting for it to get dark.

"At this point," he related, "I'm pretty relaxed, but Pete and Bill are getting jumpy."

"What about Raymond?" Nicolosi queried.

"I don't know," J.R. replied. "He's in the pizza place."

At dusk, he said, Bill and Pete left them and went behind the row of shops to change clothes and go to the Smarts' condo to wait for Gregg to come home. After about an hour he and Raymond drove along a loop road that ran

137

between the shops and the condo complex to see if there was any activity. Raymond, who knew Gregg's truck from the time he and Bill went to Derry several weeks before, said the vehicle was not in front of the condo. So they went back to the Hood Plaza lot and waited some more. It was on their second pass a half hour or so later that they connected.

"Raymond says he sees them running across the field," J.R. said, "but I didn't see them at first." After he spotted them he drove closer so he could intercept them. About that time they saw him, too, and started running toward the car. Pete tripped and fell, but Bill kept running. Bill reached the car first and scrambled in, followed seconds later by Pete. Pete yelled at him to drive off.

"Raymond asked him why and Bill said, 'We killed somebody. We killed somebody.'"

J.R. confessed that he thought they were joking, even though they were obviously nervous and frightened.

"Why did you think it was a joke?" asked Nicolosi.

"I knew why they were going there," J.R. explained. "I knew they made a first attempt. But I didn't believe they were going to do it. I figured they would take the stereo and stuff and leave before Gregg came home."

"Why didn't you believe they were going to do it?" the prosecutor pressed.

"They planned to use a knife," he said as

calmly as if he were talking about a baseball game. "And I didn't believe either one of them had the guts to kill somebody. I didn't think they really would."

The next day, he said, he and Bill were in science class when they were summoned to the office of the school's guidance counselor. Aware that they had worked with Pam in Project Self-Esteem, she said she wanted to tell them that Pam's husband had been killed.

"What was your reaction?" Nicolosi wanted to know.

J.R. looked surprised by the question. "Me and Bill acted shocked," he said, as much to say "Well, what did you expect us to do?"

Two days later he and Bill drove with the counselor to Derry to attend Gregg's wake.

"Did you speak with [Pam] at the wake?"

"Only briefly," J.R. replied. "Just for a second or two."

When asked what he expected to receive in return for his role in the murder, J.R. said he was promised five hundred dollars.

"Where was that going to come from?" asked Nicolosi.

"Insurance money," he shot back. "Pam was going to get ninety thousand dollars on one policy and fifty thousand dollars on another."

"Who told you that?"

"Bill and Pam," he said, tying Pam into the transaction. Pete had testified earlier that he had been told about payment by Bill but he'd never discussed it with Pam herself, which was not surprising considering the animosity that existed between the two. J.R., on the other hand, had a much closer relationship with Pam and by that spring saw her almost daily, usually in the presence of Bill.

"She told me after the death there probably would be an investigation so she wouldn't get the money immediately. There probably would be a wait."

In addition, he said, Bill had offered him anything of his that he wanted—"But I declined that"—plus they could use Gregg's truck and his off-road vehicle, and they could take whatever they wanted out of the condo on the night of the murder.

Did you ever actually get anything, Nicolosi asked.

"Yeah," J.R. admitted. "I got a pair of speakers from Gregg's truck."

Despite a systematic, determined approach to break J.R.'s story, Sisti had little more luck with him than he'd had with Pete.

He successfully established that the three—J.R., Pete, and Bill—were best friends (J.R. thought so much of the friendship, he said, that he would be willing to go to jail, for the rest of his life, if necessary, to preserve the union), that they had discussed the event from the very beginning, and that they continued to talk about it. But he could not make him admit that they colluded on their stories or fabricated testimony.

In fact, one part of J.R.'s testimony directly contradicted Pete's.

When he was on the stand, Pete testified that the bullet used to kill Gregg was one from a box of ammunition that had been purchased the afternoon of the killing. J.R., on the other hand, said the bullets had been purchased long before, possibly as early as March.

Hoping to use that as a wedge to break open J.R.'s story, Sisti hammered on the point.

Why did you get those kinds of bullets? Sisti asked, explaining that hollow-point shells were designed for destruction and for no other purpose, certainly not target practice.

Bill wanted them to show to Pam, J.R. said, to prove to her that he had intentions to kill her husband as she had asked.

But why that particular kind of bullet? Sisti wanted to know.

"Bill wanted *them* bullets," J.R. insisted. "He asked me what kind of bullets I thought would be best [to kill someone], and I told him."

Sisti contended that the fact that they were .38-caliber bullets indicated that they had made a decision as early as March to kill Gregg with J.R.'s father's pistol.

No, said J.R. "Back in March my father's gun wasn't even planned on being used in the murder. Back then I wasn't going to let them take the gun, and I wasn't going to take part." There had been at least three other attempts to find another firearm, J.R. said, beginning before the first attempt to kill Gregg.

According to Bill's testimony, Raymond and Bill had searched Raymond's house, looking for Raymond's father's gun, but they were never able to find it. Soon after that, Bill said he had been told by Cecelia that she knew someone who kept a pistol in his car, so Bill apparently broke into the car, searching for the weapon. He could not find it. On a third try, Cecelia pointed out for them a car that she believed contained a weapon. Again the search evidently was fruitless. J.R. said the use of his father's pistol was a last-minute decision, and even then Gregg was supposed to have been killed with a knife rather than his father's Charter Arms revolver.

Unable to make much headway in that direction, Sisti tried another approach: he decided to try to show that J.R. and the others were unfeeling about Gregg's murder.

"You didn't even care about the killing, did you?" he asked J.R. accusingly.

"Yes, I did," J.R. replied matter-of-factly.

"How did you care?"

"I was shocked," J.R. said, not sounding shocked. "It was hard to think they actually went through with it. I was scared, yes. Nervous. Upset, yes. It's not an easy thing to go through."

Did he remember telling a police officer that his first reaction was ambivalence? Sisti asked.

"Yes," J.R. responded, "but that was the first night and then it started to sink in. It was like seeing somebody being killed on TV. But the more I thought about it, the more it bothered me."

"Do you remember leaning down over his casket?"

"Yes."

"Did it bother you then?"

"Yes," J.R. said in the same even tone of voice.

Before giving up on J.R., Sisti wanted to make one more try; he wanted to try to add weight to his theory that Bill had been obsessed with Pam and that he had killed her husband out of jealousy.

"Wasn't it Bill's intention from the very beginning—from the fall of 1989—to somehow or other end up with her?"

"He said that, yes," J.R. conceded.

"He was already back then saying how he was in love with her, how he wanted Pam more than anything in the world?"

J.R. admitted that was true but explained that Bill's fixation was not as strong in the beginning as it became later. "Gradually it picked up as he began seeing her more and got to know her better. It was February when he really began talking about him and Pam."

Was that the time, Sisti asked, that he also started talking about how much he hated Gregg?

"Yes," J.R. agreed.

"You thought it was kind of strange that he was talking about her so much, didn't you? As one of his best friends, you were even trying to relax Bill, right?"

"Yes," J.R. admitted.

However, Sisti's point was weakened somewhat on redirect when Nicolosi pointed out that J.R. also began seeing more of Pam as time went by and it was not just Bill who was going to her office.

"That's right," J.R. said.

At that point in the trial, the defense strategy was clear: Try to show that Pete, Bill, and J.R. had murdered Gregg for three reasons: 1) because Bill was jealous of Gregg and wanted him out of the way; 2) because they wanted to know what it felt like to kill someone; and 3) because they wanted whatever they could steal from Pam and Gregg's condo. After the murder, they allegedly conspired to protect each other while blaming Pam for the death.

Up until then, however, Sisti had little luck in establishing any of these points. Although he questioned both Pete and Bill about Pete's alleged desire to experiment with murder, he had not scored any convincing hits. And the insistence by both Pete and J.R. that Pam had participated in the planning, even as late as the very afternoon of the murder, was powerful testimony.

The photo that Pamela Smart gave to her fifteen-year-old lover, Billy Flynn. *(AP/Wide World)*

The home of Pamela and Gregg Smart, on Misty Morning Drive in Derry. *(Tami Plyler, Sygma)*

Pamela Smart leaves the Rockingham County Courthouse in Exeter after a hearing. *(Tami Plyler, Sygma)*

Pamela Smart leaves her former home after showing jurors the scene of her husband's murder. *(Tami Plyler, Sygma)*

Billy Flynn on his way into the courtroom to plead guilty to second-degree murder. *(Tami Plyler, Sygma)*

Patrick "Pete" Randall tells jurors how Pam Smart left the door to her condominium unlocked so he and Billy Flynn could get in and murder her husband. *(AP/Wide World)*

Vance "J.R." Lattime tells jurors how he took the .38 caliber handgun from his father's bedroom so Bllly Flynn could use it to shoot Gregg Smart. *(AP/Wide World)*

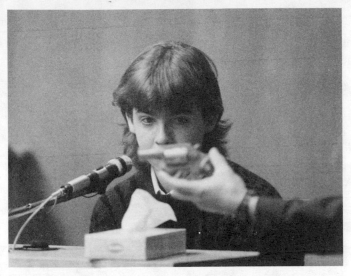
Billy Flynn is shown the gun he used to kill Gregg Smart.
(AP/Wide World)

Key witness for the prosecution, Cecilia Pierce, is sworn in.
(Tami Plyler, Sygma)

Diana Cullen *(top)* and Marianne Moses *(bottom)*, inmates at the State Prison for Women in Goffstown, testify at a hearing that Pam Smart asked them if she could hire a contract killer to silence witness Cecilia Pierce. *(Tami Plyler, Sygma)*

The attorneys for the defense, Paul Twomey and Mark Sisti.
(Tami Plyler, Sygma)

The prosecutors for the State, Paul Maggiotto and Diane Nicolosi. *(Tami Plyler, Sygma)*

The grieving parents of Gregg Smart, Judith and William Smart. *(Tami Plyler, Sygma)*

The parents of Pam Smart, Linda and John Wojas. *(Tami Plyler, Sygma)*

Pete and J.R. had come across basically as two unfeeling youths. On the other hand, Pam had sat calmly at the defense table through some exceedingly damaging testimony and never blinked any eye. Dressed every day in stylish business clothes with a bright bow or ribbon in her hair, she appeared so emotionless that journalists almost immediately dubbed her the "Ice Princess." To that point, everyone involved in the death had projected an amazing lack of emotion. But if emotion was what everyone wanted, they would get it with the next witness: Bill Flynn. He would emote to the point where Sisti and Twomey almost seemed ready to throw up their hands and cry for relief.

19

BILL'S TESTIMONY BEGAN calmly enough.

A thin, almost feminine-looking youth with shoulder-length dark hair parted down the middle and combed behind his ears, Bill had a narrow, triangular face with oversize liquid eyes that looked upward through bangs reaching to his eyebrows and a sad, almost pouty mouth. He had a DJ's voice, but he spoke so softly, so deferentially, that at times he was unintelligible. But when he began quietly filling in many of the gaps in his relationship with Pam, hardly anyone in the courtroom even coughed for fear they would miss his words.

He had become infatuated with Pam on the first day he met her, Bill said. And that was when she'd walked into a classroom where Project Self-Esteem for the 1990–91 school year was being organized. He had volunteered as a student facilitator for the program, and Pam was there as a volunteer adult facilitator. During the organizational meetings, the group broke up into smaller working crews, and Bill said he was careful to make sure he was in Pam's circle.

"I wanted to be with her because she was attractive," he confessed, adding that he had been impressed when she mentioned that she had pictures of herself with members of several heavy-metal groups, pictures that were taken during her days with the student radio station at Florida State.

As he talked, Pam, dressed in an electric blue suit with a matching bow, scribbled furiously on a white pad, apparently hearing many of his admissions for the first time.

When he told her how much he admired the heavy-metal bands she was talking about, she invited him to her office across the street to see the pictures. From there, he said, the relationship grew slowly stronger.

"I liked talking to her," he said, so low that Prosecutor Paul Maggiotto had to ask him to speak up. "We had a lot in common."

Branching out from Project Self-Esteem, just before Christmas 1990, Pam asked Bill if he wanted to get involved in a project she was directing involving an orange juice commercial. She wanted to produce a film clip to enter in a national contest. The prize was a free trip to Walt Disney World. Seizing the opportunity to see more of her, Bill readily agreed. He would be the cameraman.

From seeing her occasionally in connection with Project Self-Esteem, Bill suddenly found himself in her presence three or four days a week for two or three hours at a stretch. On top of that, he was spending most of his study periods in her office across the street from the high school, participating in what he called "brainstorming sessions" for the orange juice project. One of the other members of the small group was Cecelia Pierce.

"We became good friends," Bill said, speaking of his burgeoning relationship with Pam.

"Did you know she was married?" Maggiotto asked.

"Yes," Bill said softly.

"Did you know who she was married to?"

"Yes," he replied. "Gregg Smart."

Early in February, as his infatuation was reaching the point of obsession, Bill got a message from Pam via Cecelia: "Come to my office, there's something I want to tell you."

But when he got there, he said, she seemed reluctant to explain why he had been summoned. "She was nervous," Bill related. "She wasn't going to tell me at first."

"What was it?" Maggiotto prompted, giving Bill his head, encouraging him to take as much time as he wanted with his story.

"First she asked me if I thought about her when she wasn't around. I said yeah. And she said, 'Well, I think about you all the time.'"

"What did you think of that?" Maggiotto asked.

"I was kind of shocked," Bill replied. "I just listened. I didn't expect it. She said she didn't know what to do because she was married. But I was pretty happy. I was a fifteen-year-old kid and here was a twenty-two-year-old woman who was very attractive saying she liked me. I was a little confused."

"What happened after that?" the prosecutor asked.

The next progression occurred a few days later, Bill recalled. He said he and Pam had been out shooting scenes for the orange juice commercial and they ended up at his house. They went into his room and he closed and locked the door. They stretched out on the bed and started talking. "We were lying on top of the covers," he recalled. "My mother was home, but she was in another part of the house. Pam said, 'Do you want to kiss me?' and I said yeah. Then she said, 'Do I have to come over there and rape you?'" Then, he said, they started "making out," but they did not have intercourse. That did not occur until several days later, when he and Pam and Cecelia, who was there as a stalking horse, went to Pam's condo while Gregg was out of town on business.

"Before that," Bill said, "she asked me if I had ever seen the movie *Nine and a Half Weeks*. I told her no. She said in the movie Kim Basinger dances for Mickey Rourke and she wanted to dance like that for me."

On the way to the condo, they stopped and

picked up several movies at a video store, including *9 1/2 Weeks*.

"We watched the movie and then we went upstairs," Bill said, leaving Cecelia downstairs to watch the other movies they had brought home.

"I was sitting on the bed—"

"What were you wearing?" Maggiotto interrupted.

"I wasn't wearing anything."

"What about the defendant?"

"She was embarrassed," Bill said. "She went in the bathroom. She stuck her head out the door and said she was fat. I said, 'No, you aren't.'"

There was a portable stereo in the guest room, Bill said, and they had brought it into the main bedroom. When Pam came out of the bathroom she was wearing a negligee she had bought specifically for the occasion. She put Van Halen's album *OU812* into the player, and when the song "Black and Blue" began playing, she began to dance.

"After that we had sex," he said.

"On the bed?" Maggiotto asked.

"On the bed . . . on the floor. Everywhere," Bill replied.

At one point later in the night, he added, he went downstairs and came back with a glass full of ice cubes, which he used to rub on Pam, re-creating another scene from *9 1/2 Weeks*.

"Up to this point," the prosecutor injected,

breaking the reverie, "had you had any discussions with the defendant about her husband?"

"No," he said, shaking his head.

The first discussion, he said, came the next day. After Pam dropped Cecelia off at her house, she was driving him home when she started talking about having someone killed. He said he misunderstood at first and thought she was talking about her secretary.

"Why would you want to have her killed?" he recalled asking her.

"Not my secretary," Pam replied. "I meant Gregg."

Then, Bill recalled, she told him that the only way they could be together was to get rid of Gregg. Otherwise, he said Pam told him, he would take everything in a divorce. "She said she wouldn't have a car or furniture or a place to live because everything was in his name. She said he would even take Halen," referring to the Shih Tzu dog.

According to him, Pam said that she and Gregg had gotten married because it was the thing to do, but since then he had abused her. One day, he quoted her as saying, Gregg had thrown her out of the house into the snow.

"She started crying," he recalled. "She said the only way we could be together was if we killed Gregg. She said she wanted to be with me, but the only way she could see for us to be together was to kill Gregg."

"What did you think?" asked Maggiotto.

"I didn't think she was serious," Bill said.

One day not long after that, he said, he was in her office and she told him, "This is how we can get away with it." After that she outlined a plan that essentially was the one Bill followed later when the murder was actually committed.

Maggiotto asked if he was talking to Pete and J.R. about this at that time.

"Yes," Bill said.

"Did they offer any assistance?"

"No."

"Did you look for a gun?"

"Yes," he said, relating how he tried to get into cars fingered for him by Cecelia.

"When was the first time you tried to kill Gregg?" the prosecutor asked.

It was late in March, Bill said. Pam had a meeting that night and she said that would be a good time to do it. He told her he would try, but he had no intention of doing it.

"It was not something I wanted to do," he said. "But I didn't tell her that. I was saying, 'All right, I'll go ahead.'"

However, instead of going to the condo in Derry to attack Gregg, he went home. Later that night, after his mother went to bed, he called Pam at her office. He thought Pam would understand and the relationship would settle down and continue as it had for the last month or so.

"I told her I didn't go up. I didn't have a car or a gun. She snapped at me."

"What do you mean?" Maggiotto asked.

"She started yelling at me," he said. "She screamed, 'You don't love me. If you did, you'd do this for me so we could be together. You don't want us to be together. There's no sense going on and seeing each other like this because we're never going to be together.'"

"How did you feel?"

"I was really upset," Bill said. "I started crying."

"What was Pam's voice like?"

"I had never heard her like that."

"What did you think was going on?"

"I thought that was it," he explained; he thought the relationship was finished. But it wasn't.

The next day, he said, Cecelia approached him between classes and extended another invitation from Pam.

"I went over to see her, and she apologized for getting mad. She said not to worry, that she had another meeting coming up and we could do it then."

"After she told you that, what did you do?" Maggiotto asked.

"I said okay, I'd do it. At this time I started talking to Pete and J.R. and Raymond again. I wanted to get a gun to show her. J.R. and Pete still refused to help me. They said I was crazy."

"What about Raymond?"

According to Bill, Raymond asked what Pam had in her house that was worth stealing.

"I told Raymond what the situation was," Bill said. "I told him that Pam said if he helped me out, he could have anything in the house that he wanted. He said all right."

Before he died, Raymond's father was a police officer, Bill said, and Raymond thought his gun was still around the house somewhere. But when they searched they were unable to find it. Raymond said not to worry, that a knife would do just as well.

Together they began refining the plan. Bill collected some old sweat clothes they could wear and discard afterward. Raymond suggested that they should not wear their everyday sneakers because police could take prints and trace them. What they should do, he said, was wear some old sneakers they could throw away afterward.

Bill gathered the clothes and put them in a duffel bag, which he kept in his closet. Into the bag went a sharp knife, courtesy of Raymond.

"This is around the end of April," Bill said, "maybe a little less than a month after the first attempt. Pam had told me she would leave the bulkhead door open. But we still didn't have a car."

Pam solved that problem, too, he said, by agreeing to let them use her CRX. She left it in the parking lot behind her office with the keys in the ignition. Bill and Raymond would come get it, Bill said, after dark on the night they decided upon.

That afternoon he and Raymond went with Pete and J.R. to a mall to buy some concert tickets and then asked to be dropped off afterward at Pam's office. He especially remembered that Pete was with them, Bill said, because on the way to Pam's office they passed a car with a good-looking girl in it and Pete mooned her. "We were all laughing about that," he added.

When he got in Pam's car and turned on the ignition, he said, the cassette player began a Van Halen album. It was cued to the song "Black and Blue."

From Pam's office they drove to his house to get the duffel bag. Then, on the way out of town, they stopped at a drug store so he could get some latex gloves. "I bought six pairs," he said. "They were ten cents a pair."

On the way to Derry, he said, he started getting scared.

"Why was that?" Maggiotto asked.

"I only wanted to do it out to a certain point. I didn't want to kill Gregg."

"Then why did you go through all that planning?"

"I was afraid Pam was going to leave me if I said no."

"Did she say that?"

"No, but the first time she got so mad I just assumed she would."

When they got to a fork in the highway on the way to Derry and they were supposed to take the left one, Bill said he deliberately told Raymond to go to the right. A few minutes later he confessed that he was lost and they had to stop at a gas station to ask directions. By the time they got to the condo, Bill said, Gregg's truck was parked in front. Just to make sure, they went behind the unit and saw a light on in the bedroom.

"See, he's home," he told Raymond. "We can't do it."

They went to a pay phone in the nearby plaza, Bill said, and he called Pam and told her that Gregg had beaten them there and they had been unable to go through with the plan.

They drove back to Hampton, picked up Pam, and drove Raymond home. Pam said nothing until they dropped Raymond off. Then, Bill said, she started screaming at him again.

"She said, 'How the hell did you get lost? You've been there before. You don't love me. You got lost on purpose. If you loved me, you'd do this because you'd want to be with me.' I said that I did love her; that I loved her very much."

"Did you love her?" the prosecutor wanted to know.

"Yes, I did," he replied, tears starting to roll down his cheeks.

Looking like a father whose child has just thrown a tantrum in the mall, Maggiotto asked, "Then what happened?"

"She said she had another meeting in May. I figured that was it."

* * *

At this point, Bill said, he began talking to Pete and J.R. again.

"I told them they could have anything from the house and Pam probably would give them one thousand dollars each." That got their attention.

Bill said he then went to Pam and related what he had told Pete and J.R. When he mentioned the amount of money, her expression changed.

"Is that all right?" Bill said he asked her. According to him she said, no, that was not all right. That was what tripped a lot of people up, he quoted her as saying. People got caught, she said, when they hired someone to kill someone for them. One thousand dollars was too much, she said; five hundred would be sufficient.

"Did you convey this to Pete and J.R.?"

"Yes, I did. At that point J.R. agreed to let me use his father's gun."

Maggiotto asked if Pam was ever present when he and J.R. and Pete were discussing the plan.

He thought for a moment. "No," he said. "But one time me and Pam discussed it at the media center [Pam's office] and J.R. was there. She wasn't comfortable talking about it in front of people."

"How about Cecelia?"

"From day one we talked about it in front of Cecelia," Bill responded.

"How did you feel about Pam talking about it in front of Cecelia?"

"I didn't like it," Bill said. "I didn't trust Cecelia."

"Did you ever discuss that with the defendant?"

"Yeah."

"What did she say?"

"She said, 'Cecelia will never give me away.'"

Maggiotto asked Bill if he had ever witnessed anything that would corroborate what Pam had been telling him about her relationship with her husband.

"One time," he said. "Gregory used to call her around noontime every day. One time we were over at the school and we went back to the media center. I was there. J.R. was there. Cecelia was there. And Pam was there. And Gregg called. She put it on the speaker phone. I remember he said, 'I called fifteen minutes ago. Where the hell were you?' And she said, 'What do you care?' Then they got into a big argument and he said, 'Well, do you want a divorce?' and she said, 'Well, maybe I do,' and they hung up. Then he called back and they worked things out." Afterward she told him that was how Gregg treated her all the time.

20

TUESDAY, MARCH 12, 1991: Bill Flynn's seventeenth birthday. No cake. No candles. No good wishes. It certainly wasn't his happiest, but it undoubtedly would be his most unforgettable.

After setting the background for Bill and Pam's relationship, Maggiotto led him to the murder itself.

Just before Judge Gray recessed the court for the day on Monday, Bill had explained that the bullets used the night of the murder came from a box bought for the youths on the pretext of being needed for target practice. The money for the shells came from Pam.

Telling essentially the same story that had already been related by Pete and J.R. about driving to Haverhill to get J.R.'s grandmother's car and then driving to Derry, Bill sharpened his tale when he described how it was inside the Smart condominium.

It was dark in there, he said, and the only light they dared turn on was the one in the bathroom because that room had no outside window. But once they were in the downstairs area of the unit, they had to navigate strictly by light filtering in from outside. Although they searched in vain for a flashlight, they had to make do with what they had. "It wasn't so bad once our eyes got adjusted," Bill said.

While waiting for Gregg to arrive, he and Pete discussed unscrewing the overhead light in the foyer so nothing would happen when Gregg walked in the door and flipped the switch. After kicking the idea back and forth they decided against it, figuring if police later found an unscrewed light bulb, they would know immediately that the crime had been more than a botched robbery. "It would indicate premeditation," Bill said, using a term he remembered from his crime and punishment course.

Bill walked over to the table and picked up one of two brass candlesticks, figuring he could simply whack Gregg over the head as soon as he poked his nose inside. Having second thoughts about that idea, he distractedly put the candlestick on the floor near the door.

From there he went into the kitchen and swung up on the counter. Perched there, he had a view between the venetian blind slats into the parking lot outside. Finally Gregg arrived.

"I saw him pulling up," Bill recalled. "I ran out and said, 'Jesus, Pete, he's here. He's here.'"

Pete told him to calm down and they ran into position, except they got confused in the excitement of the moment and Bill got behind the door instead of Pete, while Pete took a position across the foyer near the stairwell.

"I heard Gregg walking up toward the door," Bill said. "I could hear the keys jangling. He opened the door. He turned the lights on and he called for Halen."

He was about one step inside the doorway, not quite far enough for Bill to slam the door shut behind him.

"He just stood there," Bill recalled. "I just stood there. And Pete just stood there."

"How long a time was it?" Maggiotto asked.

"I don't know," Bill replied. "It was quite a while."

Fearing that Gregg would suspect something, Bill lunged forward and grabbed him by the shoulders of his jacket and tried to pull him inside. But Gregg started yelling and tried to back out of the house.

"What was he yelling?" Maggiotto interrupted.

"I don't remember," Bill said.

"What happened then?"

"Pete jumped out and pushed him in. Then Pete shut off the lights and tried to shut the door, but the mat got caught. He took the mat out of the doorway and shut the door. Gregg was saying, 'What's going on? What's going on?' and I was telling him to be quiet."

Bill said he and Pete, speaking at once, ordered Gregg to his knees, a command Pete reinforced by grabbing Gregg's hair and forcing him down.

In telling the story, Bill grew increasingly upset. As he related how he and Pete had grabbed Gregg, he began hyperventilating. His rapid breathing soon gave way to tears.

"Pete was talking to him; he grabbed him by the hair."

"What was he saying?"

"I don't remember. Pete was in front of him, and I was to his left and a little behind him."

Maggiotto asked Bill to leave the witness stand and stand in front of the jury box so he could demonstrate clearly what he was talking about. When he rose, he towered over the prosecutor.

"You want me to kneel down?" Bill asked.

"Yes," Maggiotto replied. "I want you to kneel down."

As Bill knelt in front of the jury with his head slightly bowed and his hands folded meekly at his waist, in imitation of Gregg's position, he struggled to maintain his composure.

"You can return to your seat," Maggiotto commented.

Flopping back onto the witness chair, Bill began crying so hard he could not speak for several moments.

"After he got into the house," Bill sobbed once he had some control, "he wasn't struggling very much."

A bailiff wearing a maroon sports jacket

strode quickly forward, deposited a box of tissues in front of Bill, and retraced his steps. "Thank you," Bill mumbled.

"Gregg just kept asking what was going on," Bill resumed.

"What did you tell him?" Maggiotto asked.

"I just told him to shut up."

Pam sat a dozen feet away at the witness table, her eyes cast downward and her tented fingers pushed lightly to her forehead. It was the closest she had come to showing any discernible emotion.

"What happened next?" Maggiotto prompted.

"We had planned to cut his throat," Bill wept, "but we just couldn't bring ourselves to do it."

He paused to wipe his eyes and take several deep breaths. "Pete had him by the hair with one hand and the knife by his face."

Coolly Maggiotto walked across the room and extracted a long, evil-looking knife from an evidence bag by the clerk's table. Quickly crossing the room to the witness stand, he showed it to Bill.

"Is this the knife?"

Bill said that it was, hardly glancing at the weapon. The bailiff returned with a glass of water, which Bill accepted gratefully.

When they realized that they could not cut his throat, Bill said, he motioned to Pete and pointed to the gun. Pete nodded his head and Bill drew the weapon.

"I took it out," he sobbed noisily, "and I cocked the hammer back."

"Did Pete or Gregg say anything?" Maggiotto asked.

"They were still talking," Bill said softly, "but I don't remember what they were saying."

"Then what happened?"

"I cocked the hammer back and I pointed the gun at his head. I just stood there. . . ."

"For how long?"

"A hundred years, it seemed like. And I said, uhhh, 'God, forgive me. . . .'" Nearly hysterical, Bill sobbed for several long moments.

"What did you do after you said, 'God forgive me'?" the prosecutor pressed.

"I pulled the trigger," Bill replied softly.

Caught up in the drama, Judge Gray coughed loudly. "It's time for a recess," he said with a faint catch in his voice.

Following the break, Bill was more in control of himself, but he continued to sob softly and dab at his eyes.

When the prosecutor asked him how far the gun had been from Gregg's head when he pulled the trigger, Bill threatened to break down again.

He didn't remember, he responded, but it had been close.

"Why did you say, 'God forgive me'?" Maggiotto asked.

"Because it is not something . . ." Bill started to say. "Not something . . ." He paused, then blurted out: *"I didn't want to kill Gregg. I wanted to be with Pam, and this is what I had to do to be with Pam. But I didn't want to kill Gregg."*

"What happened after you shot Gregory Smart?" Maggiotto asked not unkindly.

"I ran out the back door," Bill said. "I just ran."

As he had done with the knife, Maggiotto crossed the room, rummaged in a plastic bag, and extracted a pistol.

"Is this the gun?" he said, proffering it to Bill.

"Yes," Bill sobbed.

The high drama was over, but the questioning was not. As Bill fought to regain his poise, Maggiotto dug into his stack of papers and extracted a document, which he said was the plea-bargain agreement that Bill had signed with the state some seven weeks earlier.

"Did you want to testify here today?" he asked brusquely.

"No," Bill replied. "I didn't want to testify against Pam."

"Why not?" Maggiotto asked.

"For one thing," Bill replied, "I told her I'd never tell on her. And I loved her." He pointedly did not look at the defense table. And Pam pointedly did not look at him.

To begin with, Bill said, he did not want to sign the agreement unless the same deal (the opportunity to plead to second-degree murder in return for lighter sentences; a minimum of twenty-eight years for Bill and Pete; eighteen years for J.R.) also were offered to his friends. "I got them into this," he added, "and I wouldn't testify against them."

Before he was ready to turn the witness loose, Maggiotto had several other areas to cover. And he did so methodically, working down his list and, he hoped, adding another chain around Pam's cell door.

Under unrelenting questioning by the prosecutor, Bill related how Pam had

- tried to keep their relationship secret from some people, but not from others like Cecelia, Pete, and J.R.
- told him she wanted to give him a gold nugget bracelet for his birthday the previous March 12, but that Gregg would have freaked out if he had seen five hundred dollars missing from the checking account. Instead she gave him a subscription to *Guitar* magazine in Cecelia's name
- appeared shocked when he and J.R. appeared at Gregg's wake; pulling him aside, she said that she could not believe that they had come, and when they walked through the door she felt like "shitting bricks"
- told him how she had been unable to cry the night of Gregg's murder and sought solace only in her dog, Halen
- accused Bill of not loving her and threatened to break off the relationship because he had refused to fetch her a lollipop when he, Pete,

J.R., and J.R.'s girlfriend had been helping her shop for a new car
- never asked him what had happened in the condo the night of May 1, 1990 ("I didn't want her to know, and she didn't want to know")
- anonymously returned to Bill's mother, after his arrest, an audio tape he had made for her the day after they first made love

One of the most poignant tales of all that Bill told, however, excluding his rendition of Gregg's murder, was the one about the events that transpired the day before he, Pete, and J.R. were arrested.

After Pete and J.R. had come to Pam's condo and told them about Ralph Welch's apparent intentions to go to the police, the three youths felt they had to make a move. Climbing into Pam's CRX, they asked her to drive them to Seabrook, where J.R. had to get something from his house. While he went to get whatever it was he felt he needed, Bill and Pete waited at a small store a quarter mile away. Pam, seeing Cecelia's mother in another store nearby, dropped them off and then came back to pick them up.

As they were driving back to her condo, the three teenagers discussed their bleak future, commenting that the police might be looking for them even at that moment. When she heard that, Pam braked the car to a stop and ordered them out. "I don't want anything to do with you if the cops are coming," she said.

They refused to leave the car, so she continued to the condo. When they got there, Pete and J.R. climbed aboard their motorbike and said they were going to get Pete's mother's car and come back to pick up Bill.

"Not here you're not," Pam said, telling them they could pick up Bill at Winnacunnet High because she didn't want to take the chance that they might lead the police to her doorstep.

After his friends had left, Bill told Pam good-bye.

"Don't worry," he said he told her. "You'll never be brought up [arrested]."

You're only juveniles, he remembered her telling him, and the longest you would be locked up would be until you were eighteen.

Without comment, Maggiotto took his seat. Bill relaxed, apparently forgetting for the moment that the roughest part of his testimony might be yet to come: his cross-examination.

21

IT SHOULD NOT have been surprising to anyone that Maggiotto seemed just shy of hostile with Bill. It was a prosecutor's job to send lawbreakers to prison, and by every definition Bill fit that description. The teenager had come into a courtroom and described, under oath and in graphic detail, how he had murdered a man whose apparent bad luck it had been to be married to a woman who wanted him dead and had the determination to accomplish that end.

Although Bill was testifying for the state, helping to put away the person the prosecutor felt was *really* responsible for Gregg Smart's death, Maggiotto did not feel under any obligation to feel sympathy for the killer, even if he had been just a tool. In fact, when he had gone over Bill's plea-bargain agreement with him, Maggiotto made it clear that although Bill was entitled under law to ask for a further reduction of the agreed-upon sentence, the state could, and would, oppose such a move if one was ever initiated. Just because an agreement had been drafted, Maggiotto pointed out, it was by no means a done deal; it still had to be approved by a judge. In addition, if the attorney general's office felt that Bill, Pete, or J.R. was reneging on the agreement, they could ask a grand jury to indict them for first-degree murder, which carried a sentence of life without parole.

Bill may have been Maggiotto's star witness, but it was a marriage of convenience. Bill needed to testify for the prosecution to help secure his plea bargain, and Maggiotto had to dance with him to get the person he really wanted: Pam.

While Maggiotto had to be at least civil to Bill, the defense was under no such constraint. It was the *duty* of Pam's attorneys to be as abrupt as necessary with Bill, as remorseless and unsparing as possible, to accomplish their aim—which was to destroy Bill's credibility as a witness against Pam and demolish him in the eyes of the jurors.

Without preliminary, when his turn came, Mark Sisti launched his attack against Bill with what court watchers had come to recognize as his favored prefix for virtually every question: "Tell the jury . . ."

"Bill, can you tell the jury whether or not you had lunch on May 2, 1990?"

If the approach was designed to catch the witness off guard, it worked to a certain degree. The question certainly wasn't what Bill expected.

"Honestly, no," he said after a puzzled pause. "I don't remember."

The query about whether Bill had a sandwich with a school chum seemed to come out of the blue. If Bill had admitted that he had lunched with that person and that he had indeed picked up the tab, Sisti could have pounced with the question he really wanted to ask: Was it financed by money stolen from Gregg Smart?

It would have made a good picture for the jury: a new image of the witness who had just broken down on the stand, laughing and chowing down hours after a murder and using the victim's cash to pay for the occasion. But by saying he didn't remember, Bill forced Sisti to follow a more circuitous route to get to the same place—which in this case was nowhere. When, three questions later, Sisti asked Bill if he remembered stripping Gregg's wallet, Bill said he did not. Nor did he remember Pete committing any such act.

"So that wallet is just lying on the floor for no reason at all?" he asked.

"I'm sure there is a reason," Bill replied.

How about Gregg's ring? Sisti wanted to know, returning to a point he had pushed Pete on six days earlier. But the defense attorney had no more success with Bill than he had with Pete. Bill denied any knowledge about the ring.

Sisti suggested that Bill take another look at

the photograph of Gregg stretched out on the foyer hall. This may have been Sisti's true reason for bringing up the wallet; he could not have helped but notice how the picture had affected Bill earlier, and his aim may have been to unnerve him some more, using the question about the wallet as a lead-in to showing him the photograph. Pam had bragged to Cecelia earlier that her lawyers, though expensive, were good.

"What's in that photograph?" Sisti asked.

"A wallet, a ring, and some keys."

"Can you tell this jury that you didn't go through Gregg's wallet?"

Bill looked at the jury box. "I'm telling the jury that if I did, I don't remember. I wasn't in a very calm state of mind."

"What were you? In a frenzy or something?" Sisti snapped.

"I was scared to death," Bill said quietly.

The defense lawyer asked him if he remembered "ripping" a ring off Gregg's finger or seeing Pete do it.

When Bill said no, Sisti turned abruptly to Bill's earlier dramatic display of emotion, hinting that it may have been simulated.

Did he cry when he shot Gregg in the head? Did he cry when he ran out the back door and escaped? Did he cry on the drive back to Seabrook?

Bill answered "No" each time.

"Were you laughing at the song?" he asked,

referring to J.R.'s testimony about singing a non-sense ditty to try to calm Bill down.

"I don't think I was," Bill said. "I don't remember that night very well."

Sisti leaped. "You don't *remember* the night you killed Gregg Smart very well?" he asked, his voice dripping with sarcasm.

"I *remember* it," Bill said. "I just don't remember how I was trying to deal with it. I was scared."

Turning to another theme he had worked with Pete and J.R., Sisti tried to get Bill to admit that the real reason he had killed Gregg was that he was jealous of him and that he hated Gregg because he was married to Pam.

Bill answered that his anger toward Gregg was directed to the fact that Gregg abused Pam rather than a result of jealousy.

"Pam told me he used to hit her. She said he used to grab her by the hair and throw her down." He had seen a bruise on her arm, he said, a tan, yellowish mark on the upper left portion of her arm, which Pam said had come from Gregg.

"Did it anger you when you saw that bruise?" Sisti asked.

"Yes, it did," agreed Bill.

When Bill couldn't pin down when he had seen the mark, Sisti implied that it was a figment of Bill's imagination.

"She showed the bruise to Cecelia, too," Bill

contended. "I didn't see Gregg hit her, so I can't say it was a bruise from Gregg Smart. But, yes, it *was* a bruise."

Sisti also tried to capitalize on the confusion over when the box of bullets was purchased that included the round that killed Gregg. Pete had said they were bought the afternoon of the murder. J.R. said he thought he had them for more than a month. Bill testified in response to a question from Maggiotto that they had been bought two days before the murder. Under Sisti's cross-examination he wavered on his earlier statement, admitting he was vague on the date, but he was certain that it was within a week of the killing.

Sisti put a lot of emphasis on the bullets because their purchase indicated that Bill had planned long before he said he did to shoot and kill Gregg. The fact that Bill had admitted to trying to steal a gun as early as March proved that he wanted to kill Gregg almost as soon as he started sleeping with Pam.

"I wanted to steal the gun," said Bill, who proved quick on his feet, "but not to kill Gregg." He wanted it, he said, to show to Pam so she would think he was doing what she wanted and would ease up in her demands that he murder her husband.

"I never would have killed Gregg if it were not for Pam," he insisted.

"You're telling this jury that the only reason

you killed Gregg is because you loved Pam? Is that what you're saying?"

"No," Bill responded quickly, saying he killed Gregg because Pam asked him to. And he loved Pam.

"And you would do whatever Pam told you to do? Is that what you're saying?"

"Yes," Bill agreed. "I probably would back then."

"Kind of like you had no brain at all," Sisti barked, hoping to get a heated reaction.

"I had a brain," Bill said calmly. "But I was in love."

"You're saying somebody made you kill Gregg," Sisti persisted.

"I would not have killed Gregg if Pam had not wanted me to," Bill answered, refusing to be drawn in.

"You're saying that Pam made you kill Gregg?"

"Yes."

"And that act was not really you?"

"I performed the act, yes, but I would not have done it if Pam had not told me to."

"You're just a machine or something like that?"

"It was the first girl I ever loved," Bill said. "I didn't want her to leave me."

Before abandoning his efforts to shake Bill's stance, Sisti had one more card he wanted to play.

Questioning Bill about his course work at

Winnacunnet High, Sisti established that one of the classes Bill had been taking that spring was called crime and punishment, where part of the classwork included dramatizations in which the students played various roles in a crime situation motif.

At the time he, Pete, and J.R. were planning to kill Gregg, Bill and J.R. had been assigned the roles of terrorists in the classroom playlet. According to the script, the characters portrayed by Bill and J.R. had announced plans to kill a hostage for every day their demands went unheeded.

It was, Sisti pointed out, a very handy scenario, one that he hinted had been devised by Bill and J.R. as a reflection of their true characters.

Bill denied that he had played any part in developing the characters or deciding which roles he and J.R. would fill.

It had been an interesting move by Sisti, one he apparently had hoped would strike some sort of chord in Bill and lead him to possibly damaging admissions.

When it failed to have the desired effect, Sisti shrugged in resignation, as if to say he had given it his best shot. Although his strategy produced few results on Bill (as it also had on Pete and J.R.), there was always the next witness, and that was one the defense was particularly anxious to question: Cecelia Pierce.

22

BEFORE THEY COULD get to Cecelia, however, there were a few more witnesses called by Nicolosi and Maggiotto to help substantiate what had been testified to so far. The prosecutors had dumped a lot of raw data on the jury all at once, and now Nicolosi and Maggiotto wanted to go back and tie up a few loose ends before getting to the one person they hoped would *really* sink Pam Smart: Cecelia Pierce.

Elaine Flynn, Bill's mother, testified that she had a strong suspicion that Bill was romantically involved with the beautiful young school official, but her misgivings grew from an incident involving a roll of film more than from anything her son had told her.

Bill, she said, had been distant ever since his father had been killed, and the two of them were not close; he did not confide in her. But she had a feeling something was going on when a family friend who ran a photo-finishing business brought her a set of photographs that had been picked up by her son. The pictures showed two bikini-clad women in suggestive poses. One of the women was Pam Smart.

During his testimony the previous day, Bill had said the pictures dated to a time before his sexual involvement with Pam. It was during the orange juice commercial days, he said, and Pam had casually mentioned that she had some film that needed processing. Bill told her he had a friend who had a photo-finishing business and he could get her a discount.

He picked up the film and returned it to her, but he said she was unhappy with the results and was going to throw the photographs away when she offered them to him instead. Bill, who had admitted under cross-examination that he had wanted to sleep with Pam from the first time he saw her, eagerly accepted the pictures.

Elaine Flynn said the only other indication she had that her son and Pam were romantically linked came when Bill told her, just before his arrest, that he was in a lot of trouble.

"I didn't know if he was involved or was being set up," she said on the stand. "I was in a panic."

Except for meeting her briefly on the occasions when Bill brought her to the house, Flynn said her only other contact with Pam occurred on the morning after Bill's arrest. A semihysterical Pam called her, she said, demanding information about what was happening in the case.

"I told her," Flynn said, "that I couldn't believe

what was going on and she had better get a lawyer."

In addition to the pictures, Bill had admitted under questioning from Maggiotto that he and Pam had written a series of "love letters" to each other during the time of their affair, usually brief notes of endearment, although at least one of them was sexually explicit.

Almost all of the dozen or so letters were later destroyed. The letters, however, were an open secret among a group of Bill's friends. J.R. had testified earlier that Bill used to slip him the notes to read during crime and punishment class. Bill also admitted sharing the letters with Pete and with Sarah Thomas, a girl Bill had known since junior high.

Sarah testified that murder was not mentioned in any of the letters she had seen, although they were undeniably romantic and titillating. In one of them, she said, Pam was angry because Bill had kissed another girl after a Mötley Crüe concert about two weeks before the murder.

"Did you ever ask Bill Flynn if he was in love with Pam Smart?" Sisti asked Sarah.

"Yes," she replied. "I asked him that. He said he didn't know about love, but the sex was great."

Ralph Welch, the teenager who had helped precipitate the arrests of Bill, Pete, and J.R., testified that he had felt "sick" and "shocked" when he learned that his three friends had planned and executed a murder.

"I couldn't believe it," he said. "I really didn't want to. I couldn't believe that my best friends would kill someone."

He learned about the incident, he said, through another friend, Daniel Blake, who was a cousin of Raymond Fowler. Blake told him, Ralph said, that someone should talk to Raymond about comments he was making regarding the murder.

It was at that point that Ralph went to Pete and J.R., with whom he was living at the time, and asked if it was true. When they denied it, he eavesdropped outside J.R.'s door and heard them talking about the murder. When he confronted them again, Pete took him outside and filled him in on what had happened.

On the stand, Ralph said that Pete had calmly told him that Gregg was "worth more dead than alive" and that Gregg "never even saw it coming."

After going to the police with J.R.'s father, Ralph drove to Maine, where Raymond was staying, to warn him about what was about to happen. He said he also wanted him to be prepared in case Bill, Pete, and J.R. came looking for him seeking revenge for apparently setting the entire process in motion.

"I didn't want another person to get killed,"

Ralph said, explaining why he had gone to warn Raymond.

He also told how he had received a telephone call from Bill on the Sunday morning after he had learned about the murder—after he and Pete had fought in front of J.R.'s house because Ralph told Pete not to come around anymore.

The call from Bill, made from Pam's condo, was designed to keep Ralph from going to the authorities. During the call, Ralph said, Bill pleaded with him not to tell because it would be the end of his relationship with Pam. Bill had admitted telling Ralph that Pam meant everything to him and that if he lost her, he would kill himself.

According to Ralph, Bill denied the murder, saying, "You know I wouldn't do anything like that."

Unimpressed, Ralph said he replied, "I know you did do it."

Under cross-examination by Paul Twomey, Pam's second defense attorney, Ralph said the tale he heard about the murders did not involve Pam except that Pete and J.R. were supposed to get five hundred dollars each out of the insurance money she was going to receive after Gregg's death.

He added, however, that J.R. had proudly shown him the speakers he said had come from Gregg Smart's truck. Rather than saying the speakers had been given to him in partial payment for his participation in the murder, however, J.R. told him that he was buying the speakers from Pam on an installment plan.

At one point before the murder, he said, Bill had laughingly mentioned that he was going to "do Gregg."

Twomey, wanting to make sure the jury caught Ralph's statement that Bill was laughing when he said it, tried to get Ralph to elaborate.

"He wasn't overcome with grief as he told you this?" Twomey asked, referring to Bill.

"No," Ralph said. "He was laughing. That's why I didn't take him seriously."

"Were tears coming from his eyes?"

"No," Ralph replied.

Ralph, Sarah, and Elaine Flynn were the last witnesses before Cecelia was scheduled to appear. Earlier, Judge Gray had refused to allow into evidence several statements from Raymond on the grounds that the statements the prosecutors wanted to present were contradicted by other statements Raymond had made. Gray said if he allowed some and not others, it would be a violation of Pam's "right to fundamental fairness guaranteed by the due process clause." Raymond himself would not appear because he was charged separately and had pleaded not guilty. If he testified in Pam's trial, he could jeopardize his own trial.

23

CECELIA'S REPUTATION preceded her.

Before the jury saw her, they heard her on the tapes: static-filled, sometimes barely audible recordings of such uneven quality that one had to be discarded altogether.

When Maggiotto was ready to present the tapes in court, headphones were handed out, along with copies of the transcript, so jurors could follow along with their eyes and thus better comprehend what they could not always follow with their ears.

All told, the tapes that became a significant part of the evidence in the case covered some seventy-nine minutes of time, less than most movies. The first thirteen and three-quarters minutes were composed of two telephone conversations on Tuesday, June 19, one week and one day after the arrests of Bill, Pete, and J.R., who were referred to collectively as "the boys" by Cecelia during her testimony. The first telephone call (at five minutes before two in the afternoon) was initiated by Cecelia, the second (at four minutes after five) by Pam. The first was the longer by almost a minute.

However, the bulk of the recordings—sixty-five minutes' worth—were made in two sessions of almost equal length when Pam and Cecelia were face to face. One session took place in Pam's office on Thursday, July 12, and the other occurred the next day in the parking lot outside. The former began at one minute before one in the afternoon and the latter at ten minutes before one.

On paper, the transcripts covered eight pages, six pages, thirty-two pages, and thirteen pages, respectively. The difference in typed length between the last two apparently was due to the fact that the first face-to-face meeting contained considerably more back-and-forth conversation while the second had more sustained dialogue, especially by Pam, which took up less space when transcribed.

In the end, the tapes were immeasurably more incriminating for Pam than Cecelia's testimony.

An overweight, sullen girl with stringy blond hair and a perpetual smirk on her round face, Cecelia was a junior at Winnacunnet High and two months shy of her seventeenth birthday when Maggiotto called her to the stand on Friday, March 15, the day after the jury heard the tapes. Clad in a blue dress with tiny white flowers, Cecelia sat for much of the time with her head cocked to one side and a half smile on lips. She answered a disturbing percentage of the questions put to her by both Maggiotto and Sisti with "I don't remember," "I don't know," "I'm not sure," or "I just said that." She was especially vague on dates other than ones she had specifically memorized, much as if she had been preparing for a history quiz. Overall, she presented the demeanor of a spoiled teenager who has just been told to do the dishes and who then accomplishes the task with the air of "All right, I'll do them, but I don't like it and you'll know I don't like it." Despite her obvious attitude problem, what she had to say caught the jury's attention.

Under prosecutorial prodding, Cecelia detailed how she had first met Pam in the fall of 1989 through Project Self-Esteem. She had known Bill for at least two years at that point, and they had always been friendly, but they had never socialized much. She knew Pete and J.R. less well than she knew Bill, and she knew Raymond and Ralph Welch only on sight.

As Project Self-Esteem progressed, she and Pam became friends and Pam asked her if she would like to be her intern, a position that required Cecelia to work a minimum of six hours every week in Pam's office, mainly typing material into the computer. Because of the job, Cecelia saw Pam twice a day during the week, and once they began working on the orange juice commercial at about Christmastime, she saw her on weekends as well. They became good friends, she added, and Pam often confided in her. It was on an afternoon early in February, she said, that Pam sat her down and told her that she thought she was in love with Bill.

What did you think of that? Maggiotto asked.

"I laughed," Cecelia replied. "It was ridiculous. Pam was married. She was twenty-two. But she just kept saying over and over again that she was serious, that she thought she was in love with Bill."

A week later, Cecelia said, Pam told Bill herself.

For that week, Cecelia said, Pam agonized over the decision, arguing constantly with herself about the limited choices she saw available. According to Cecelia, Pam was indubitably attracted to Bill, but that conflicted with her marriage. Since she was more interested in Bill than in Gregg, she had only two alternatives: divorce Gregg or have him killed.

But as far as Cecelia was concerned, there was only *one* choice. "I told her to get a divorce," she said smugly.

Pam, however, did not agree. According to Cecelia, she said that if she divorced Gregg, he would take the dog and the furniture and she would be left without a secure income and no place to live.

As she continued to torment herself over the decision, the relationship with Bill took off. After Pam told him how she felt, Bill, not surprisingly, began spending considerably more time at the media center, and, Cecelia noted, "he was always smiling."

At the same time the Bill/Pam relationship was improving, the Gregg/Pam relationship was deteriorating. One day, Cecelia said, she went into the office and Pam was on the phone arguing with someone. She mouthed, "Gregg?" and Pam nodded her head in agreement. As she stood there, Cecelia said, she heard Pam heatedly discussing who was going to take the dog, Halen, and the furniture. After a few minutes, Pam slammed down the phone and announced to Cecelia that she and Gregg were going to get a divorce.

"I told her that was good," Cecelia said.

However, a few short minutes later, Pam called Gregg back and told him that she was sorry they had a fight and urged him not to call his parents and tell them about their marital problems. "She didn't want anyone to know they were having trouble," Cecelia opined.

As Cecelia told her story, Pam, wearing a peach-colored suit and an oversize black bow in her hair, sat rigidly a few feet away, as expressionless as if she had been carved out of New England marble. Sometimes she looked dispassionately at her former intern, sometimes she scribbled on the pad in front of her, and sometimes she conversed quietly with Paul Twomey, who was sitting on her immediate left.

One time soon after Pam decided to tell Bill

about how she felt about him, Pam asked Cecelia to come stay at her condo while Gregg was off at an insurance school in Rhode Island. On the second night she was there, Pam brought Bill home as well, and the three of them watched the movie *9 1/2 Weeks*, after which Pam and Bill disappeared upstairs.

A couple of hours later, Cecelia said, she was bored and went looking for them. Calling out her imminent arrival, she said, she walked into the master bedroom and found Pam and Bill on the floor. They were nude, she said, and making love. Pam was on top. Embarrassed, she retreated back downstairs and sat watching television. Later, Bill came down, filled a glass with ice cubes, and disappeared back up the stairs.

As Pam and Bill's contacts grew more frequent, Cecelia said she was drawn increasingly into the relationship, usually as a stalking horse to help keep the love affair secret from the outside world, especially those who might take the tale to Gregg. They had to be especially careful around a girl named Tracy Collins, Cecelia said, because she was the girlfriend of Gregg's best friend.

Commonly, Pam would pick Cecelia up and then they would go get Bill. Sometimes the three of them would sit in Bill's room and talk, or they would pile into Pam's CRX, a tiny two-seater, with Cecelia, sans driver's license, behind the wheel. Pam would sit on Bill's lap on the passenger seat. Then they would drive around. Sometimes they would park behind darkened office buildings and discuss deep subjects: life in general or death in particular. Gregg's death.

Seemingly driven by the intensity of the affair, Pam and Bill began talking more frequently about murdering Gregg. These conversations were carried on quite openly in front of her, Cecelia said. And when she wasn't present for the debates, Pam filled her in. At first such conversations were rather infrequent, then they increased to the point where they were taking place on a daily basis.

"What kinds of things would Pam talk about?" Maggiotto asked.

"She would tell me what was going on, what they had discussed," Cecelia said. "Things like be sure and wear dark clothes and make it look like a burglary. Things like that."

At first, Cecelia said, Pam and Bill talked about hiring someone to kill Gregg, but apparently they could not find anyone to do the job, so Pam decided that Bill would do it. It was not long after that, she added, that Bill came to her and asked if she knew where he could get a gun.

She told him her father had a gun, but Bill lost interest when she added that it was a shotgun. He was looking for a handgun.

Eager to oblige, Cecelia said a woman she worked with told her she kept a gun in her car. One night, at work, she called Bill and told him the woman was at work and it would be a good time for him to check out her car. Bill said he was coming right over. A few minutes later he showed up and apparently searched her car without finding the weapon. Later Cecelia told him where the woman lived, and he apparently searched her car a second time, again without finding the gun she allegedly kept there.

She and Pam had gotten in the habit of referring to Bill and his friends as "the boys," and Pam religiously kept her up-to-date on the plans to murder Gregg.

At one time, she said, Pam told Bill to be particularly careful not to hurt the dog when they went to kill her husband. She also specified, Cecelia contended, that the murder was not to take place in the dog's presence because she feared the animal would be traumatized by the sight of Gregg being killed.

Since she knew what was going on virtually every step of the way, Maggiotto asked, why had she not gone to the police?

"I didn't think they were serious," Cecelia answered.

"Why not?"

"Because I had known Bill for a couple of years, and I didn't think he could kill somebody. He just didn't seem like that type of person."

Cecelia said that Pam told her on May 1 (although the time of day the conversation allegedly occurred could never be pinned down) that Gregg was going to be murdered that evening.

According to Cecelia, Pam told her that the plan was for her to work late that day and attend an evening meeting. While she was in the meeting, "they" would drive to Derry to kill Gregg.

"Did she say who 'they' were?" Maggiotto asked.

"I don't remember," Cecelia said, turning vague, as she did consistently throughout her testimony when pressed for specifics.

What, Maggiotto asked, was *her* understanding of who 'they' were?

"Bill, Pete, J.R., and possibly Raymond," she responded.

Cecelia said she saw Pam again later that day, at about seven P.M., when she and her boyfriend of the moment, Michael Welch, stopped by her office on their way to dinner. She said she and Pam talked for a few minutes, but the murder was not mentioned.

"How did you learn about the killing?" Maggiotto asked.

She was told the next morning by the guidance counselor at Winnacunnet High, she said.

And how did she react?

She was shocked, she claimed, because she didn't think they actually would do it. She added that Bill and Pete, who were told at the same time, merely "acted shocked."

When Maggiotto asked her again why she had not gone to the police, Cecelia replied that she was frightened. "I was afraid I was in trouble because Pam had told me I would be."

The next time Cecelia saw Pam was at the wake, but it was only a brief encounter. She didn't stay long at the service because Pam pulled her aside and told her that her presence there was making her uncomfortable. She would appreciate it, Cecelia quoted her as saying, if she would ask the guidance counselor to take her, Bill, and J.R. back to Seabrook. A few minutes later they left, she said.

About a week later Pam came back to work, but by that time Cecelia said *she* was uncomfortable and wanted to spend as little time around Pam as she could. "I was trying to avoid her," she admitted. "I wanted to avoid the whole situation."

Nevertheless, she said she and Michael stopped by Pam's condo on the night of June 10 after a concert. To her surprise, they found Pam extremely agitated. Asking Cecelia to come upstairs with her, Pam filled her in on how Ralph had overheard Pete and J.R. talking about the murder and how Ralph was believed to have gone to the police. She added that Bill, Pete, and J.R. had "run," and she didn't know what to do.

"She appeared to be nervous," Cecelia said. "She was talking fast and she was shaking."

Pam asked her if she would spend the night with her, and she agreed. Michael went home, but Cecelia had to go with him to retrieve her purse, so Pam followed in her CRX. On the way back to Pam's, Cecelia said, she was at the wheel when they were pulled over by a small army of police officers. Looking around, she saw a paddy wagon, two or three marked cruisers, and several motorcycle policemen. As they sat there wondering what was happening, a spotlight suddenly cut through the dark, blinding them temporarily. "I asked them why they had stopped us," Cecelia said.

The officer walked off to confer with another policeman, and when he returned a few minutes later he said there had been a mistake, that they had pulled over the wrong car. Pam and Cecelia were free to go.

The next day, Cecelia said, she was at a friend's house after school when her mother called and told her the police were anxious to interview her. She went to the police station in Seabrook and was surprised to find Pam in the parking lot. Pam told her that she wanted to go in with her, and she waited in an anteroom while Cecelia was questioned by a detective from Derry. Cecelia confessed to Maggiotto that she did not tell investigators what she knew about Gregg's murder or the circumstances leading up to it.

Despite her silence, Cecelia said, Captain Loring Jackson suspected she knew considerably more than she was telling. Before she left, she said, Jackson told her that if he found out she had been lying to him, he would seek to have her indicted for hindering an investigation.

"I was scared," she said. But she still did not reveal what she knew.

From what could be pieced together later,

Cecelia was interviewed several hours before Pete, Bill, and J.R. were arrested at a Seabrook theater. But Cecelia said she did not know this at the time.

Asked if Pam expressed her feelings about the situation, Cecelia replied that Pam told her that Bill had promised her he would not reveal her participation. She believed he would remain silent because he loved her and would not want her hurt. Also, Pam added, if Bill said anything to implicate her, he would be as good as admitting the murder himself.

24

IT WAS NOT LONG, however, before Cecelia had second thoughts about telling the police herself. It took her only four days after "the boys" were arrested.

Just before midnight on June 15, her mother called Captain Jackson and set up a rendezvous at a Dunkin' Donuts in Seabrook. When they got there, however, the restaurant was closed, so they went to another one nearby. Over coffee, Cecelia told them what she knew about the murder. When she finished, they all drove to Derry, where Cecelia repeated her statement on videotape and Jackson asked her if she would be willing to help in the investigation. It was then, she said, that she agreed to have her telephone line tapped and to wear a body mike when she talked with Pam.

Soon after her July 12–13 conversations with Pam, Cecelia said she left for a summer trip to Missouri and did not return for two weeks. When she got back on July 30, she discovered that Pam was frantic to talk to her. So she called her and said she had been out of town and would call her the next day.

On August 1 she had another brief conversation with Pam, which was taped, but Judge Gray found the quality so poor he decided not to make the jury struggle with it. The conversation, in any case, was brief and consisted mainly of Cecelia telling Pam she would see her soon. She never did because a few hours later Pam was arrested.

Anxious to get Cecelia's version of what happened after Pam's arrest on the record before the defense did, Maggiotto asked Cecelia if she had been contacted by the media.

Indeed she had, Cecelia admitted. She had appeared on the syndicated television shows "A Current Affair" and "Hard Copy" and was paid for both appearances, $300 by the former and $1,000 by the latter. After those two shows, she had so many calls from producers anxious to make a movie of her saga that she and her parents had to hire a lawyer to sift through the offers.

In the end they agreed to accept a bid from a company called Once Upon a Time Productions, which paid her $2,000 for an option on a possible movie. If the movie was ever made, Cecelia said, she would get an additional $100,000, which would be put in a trust fund. She would not be able to touch the money until she was twenty-one, which would be in May 1995.

Before turning her over to the defense, there were two more issues Maggiotto wanted to clarify. Had she talked to "the boys" about the murder since it happened? he asked. Or had she visited any of them when they were being held in the juvenile detention facility? She answered no to both questions.

One thing Maggiotto did *not* ask her, which Sisti most definitely would, was why she had not initially told police about her efforts to help Bill find a pistol.

At first, Sisti came across as amiable Uncle Mark.

"Are you comfortable?" he asked Cecelia solicitously as he spread his notes on the podium. With Pete, J.R., and particularly Bill, the defense attorney had evidenced no such concern for their physical comfort and had jumped immediately into a series of harsh questions. But with Cecelia he was walking a fine line. J.R., Bill, and Pete were self-admitted killers, but Cecelia was not. Some people, in fact, although he definitely was not one of them, considered her something of a heroine. Although that opinion did not figure largely in his strategic calculations—after all it was his *job* to help his client by verbally attacking her enemies—he nevertheless had to be careful. It would not look good to members of the jury, some of whom might have sixteen-year-old daughters of their own, for him to appear to be bullying a teenager who had helped solve a vicious crime. After all, had it not been for Cecelia, Pam might never have been brought to trial.

Treading gingerly, Sisti questioned Cecelia about her version of how she had helped Bill find a gun.

"Bill said he was looking for a firearm to kill Gregg for Pam. Is that what Bill told you?"

"No," she said, proving her alertness. "That's what *Pam* told me."

Sisti nodded, accepting the distinction. "Did he say he wanted a firearm to show to Pam?" he asked.

"No," she repeated. "He just wanted a firearm."

"He wanted to get that firearm to kill Gregg Smart, right?"

"*For Pam,* yes."

"Not just to show it to her to placate her?"

"No," Cecelia answered emphatically.

At that point Sisti seemed to make a decision. His avuncular approach was getting him nowhere. What Cecelia had done was going to go a long way toward putting a noose around his client's neck, and he wasn't going to convince the jury to be skeptical about her testimony without smashing her smugness. The set of his jaw proclaimed an end to his Mr. Nice Guy stance.

"When you had this heart-to-heart truthful

conversation with the police," he began in a noticeably rougher tone, "did you tell them about this attempt to get a firearm?"

"I don't remember," she replied, backpedaling.

Knowing by her own testimony on direct that she had not, Sisti moved in, asking her when she *did* tell them about it.

"As soon as I remembered it, I told them," she answered evasively.

"Like forty-eight hours later?"

"I don't remember."

Well, Sisti asked, *who* had she told so he might be able to get a fix on *when* she had reported it?

"I'm not sure," she said.

How long has the attorney general's office known about this phase of her involvement, he asked?

"I'm not sure," she replied.

In that case, he said, taking another tack, what was the name of the woman whose car Bill allegedly broke into in his effort to find a gun?

Cecelia said she didn't know. Since then, she explained, the woman had married and moved away. She said she did not know either her married name or where she was living.

Sisti grunted.

Anxious to impress upon the jury how cunningly Cecelia had—at least in his view—tried to hide her involvement in the attempt to secure a pistol, Sisti asked her if she had mentioned the incidents in a deposition she had given to another attorney the previous September, long before there was sufficient pressure on J.R., Pete, and Bill to convince them to plead guilty to second-degree murder. The defense attorney wanted to get her to admit that she had deliberately tried to conceal her involvement because she did not want to be charged herself.

"I think so," Cecelia said, chewing her lip.

From his pile of papers, Sisti produced a document that he said was a copy of the deposition. "Did you tell that attorney *under oath* whether or not you were involved in an attempt to secure a firearm for Bill Flynn?"

"I don't remember."

Handing her his copy of the document, Sisti invited her to peruse it and point out to him where she had made such an admission.

After several minutes of thumbing through the papers, she looked up at him and glared. He strode over and took the paper from her hand. "You didn't tell her in this deposition, did you?" he asked, stomping away.

"I guess not," she said.

Cecelia wished Sisti would fall through a hole in the floor and disappear forever; Sisti hoped he could put the squeeze on her enough for the jury to recognize her as the duplicitous young woman he was convinced she was. They responded to their desires in ways that suited their personalities and the situation. Cecelia found refuge in ambiguity, Sisti in attacking from another front.

"Did you tell the folks at 'A Current Affair' about trying to get a firearm?" he asked. "Did you tell the folks at 'Hard Copy,' when you were talking about how you couldn't sleep between June 19 and July 12 and how you rolled around in your bed, about a firearm?"

She admitted she had not.

Nodding in satisfaction, Sisti asked Cecelia if the attorney general's office had told her that her lapse in reporting this involvement was going to be covered over with a wink and a smile.

"No," she replied, adding in response to Sisti's next question that she had not been promised immunity by the prosecutors.

"Do you think you're going to be arrested?" Sisti asked.

"I don't know," she answered. "I asked the police and they said I wasn't going to be."

Under Sisti's probing, she said she had inquired about her status just a few days before she was called to testify, and Captain Jackson had told her that unless new evidence was developed showing she was more involved than she had eventually admitted to, she would not be charged.

Clearly insinuating that he did not agree with that decision, Sisti continued hammering on that theme.

"Was it your understanding that the firearm was supposed to be utilized in the killing of Gregory Smart?"

"Yes," she answered somewhat hesitantly, "but I didn't think they were going to kill him."

Sisti jumped on her use of the plural. "So now it's '*they*,'" he said. "Now it's Bill *and* Pam, while before lunch it was all Bill."

Cecelia replied she had said "they" because when she first told Bill about the gun in the woman's car, it had been in Pam's office and Pam had been present.

Sisti wanted the jury to believe that Cecelia went to the police because she was afraid she was going to be arrested as well and—later— because she saw an opportunity to profit considerably from the situation.

On June 11, he pointed out, when she had first been questioned by investigators, she had simply lied to them and had only told them the truth because she thought the net was closing around her, too. Between the time Bill, Pete, and J.R. were arrested, he wanted to know, had she also heard rumors that there was going to be another teenager—a female—picked up, too?

"Yep," she answered, tight-lipped.

"Did this make you nervous?"

"Yeah," she confessed.

"So then," he said, "you go to the police and tell them that Pam had planned the murder and she is the one they should be looking for. And then you tell them that you had nothing to do with it, right?"

"I told them what I had to do with all of it except for the gun."

Sisti leaned forward and said, his voice rising, "*'Except for the gun'!* All right!" He felt he had made a significant point.

Sisti asked how, given her knowledge of events as they transpired, she could possibly have been surprised when the murder actually took place.

"On May 1 Pam sat down with you and said, 'There's going to be a murder tonight,' but then you say you were surprised when it happened. Now does that mean you didn't believe Pam?"

"No," Cecelia answered quickly. "It means that *Pam* thought it was going to happen, but *I* did not believe the boys were going to do it."

Score one for Cecelia.

Sisti asked Cecelia why, if she had blamed everything on Pam and "the boys," she still was worried that she might be arrested.

"Because I knew somebody was going to be murdered before it happened," she replied.

"You honestly believed somebody was going to be murdered?"

"No," she said, "but it happened."

Like a fighter hearing the bell, Sisti wanted one more punch before returning to his corner.

"What it comes down to," he said, more statement than question, "is that you've got a shot at a hundred thousand dollars?"

"Yes."

"And you've already been paid what?"

"About thirty-three hundred."

"And you've been told that you're not going to be arrested?"

"Well," she replied weakly, "they didn't grant me immunity or anything."

Sisti threw up his hands, gave the jury a look that said "And what else could she ask for?" and returned to his seat.

Cecelia was the last major prosecution witness. With her, Maggiotto and Nicolosi had finished the basic outline of their presentation. There still were a few loose ends to be tied up, but not long after Cecelia shouldered her way out of the courthouse, Maggiotto rose and announced that the prosecution was complete. It was now the defense's turn.

Although there had been considerable debate in the media and among the spectators about whether Pam would take the stand, Twomey and Sisti had no hesitation about swearing her in. The prosecution's presentation had been powerful and pervasive. J.R. and Pete had been chillingly effective in their studied disinterest, and Bill had brought tears to a number of eyes when he broke down on the stand and repeatedly, tearfully, claimed that he had not *wanted* to kill Gregg, but it was the only way he could see of keeping Pam's affection. The weak link in the prosecution's case was Cecelia, who seemed to have made a less than favorable impression upon the jury with her attitude and the virtual admission that she had been motivated by other than selfless interests. But it was not her testimony that Maggiotto and Nicolosi wanted the jury to remember: it was Pam's own words elicited by Cecelia on tape that was most damaging of all.

Seemingly the only chance the defense had of successfully refuting the accusations, after the jury heard the surreptitiously recorded conversations, was for Pam to explain in her own words how those statements should be interpreted. If anybody could convince the jury that the statements were not at all what they seemed, it would have to be Pam herself.

25

WHEN PAM TOOK THE STAND on Monday, March 18, the face she presented was quite different from what most of the trial watchers expected. Although she had been physically present in the courtroom throughout the proceedings, she had been there mainly as an attractive decoration, a stylish backdrop to the drama that was taking place a few feet away on the witness stand.

Those in the courtroom and thousands on television had watched as the beautiful young blonde in her conservatively cut suits briskly entered or exited the room with her head high, or as she whispered quietly with Twomey or Sisti. But when she raised her right hand to be sworn in and took a seat, facing her accusers defiantly, her demeanor was not what most had been expecting.

She was clad as usual in executive-woman fashion: a high-collared, pleated white blouse with a tiny gold cross dangling around her neck and a navy blue suit cut on severe, almost para-military lines. The front of her jacket was broken on each side by three parallel rows of bounded pockets edged in white. When she wiggled onto her chair and turned her composed gaze out-ward, her mouth was set in such a straight, firm line that it looked like a seventh pocket. Her hair tumbled over her shoulders and spread out in bangs on her forehead. In the back, it was held in place by the ubiquitous matching bow. Her makeup was so artfully applied that it appeared virtually nonexistent.

Physically she was pure Pam, exactly what everyone had come to know and count on, the outwardly prim and proper ingenue who would have blended perfectly on any TV anchor desk anywhere in the country. But it was her voice that was the big surprise; those expecting a pol-ished, sultry-voiced seductress à la Kathleen Turner in *Body Heat* were in for a shock. When Pam spoke it was in a rapid, high-pitched, little girl voice that made her sound as much like a teenager as any of the young witnesses that pre-ceded her. But the court was interested in *what* she had to say, not *how* she said it. And her story was so significantly different from the tales told by others that it carried its own series of sur-prises.

Pam began by explaining that she had mar-ried Gregg because she loved him and that she had wanted to spend the rest of her life with him. He was, she said, her face clouding in apparent pain, a kind, gentle man who was fun to be around.

In a burst of ostensible candor, she admitted that they had a few problems in their marriage, problems that began shortly before Christmas in 1989. Her bubble burst, she said, one night in December—she didn't remember the exact date—when Gregg did not come home.

She had had a tough day, she recalled, and had gone to bed early, about ten P.M. Gregg had not yet returned from an appointment, but she thought nothing of the fact. It was only the next morning, when her alarm went off shortly after six and she realized that Gregg had not slept in the bed, that she became anxious. As she was bustling to get ready for work, she said, Gregg walked through the door. Where had he been? she asked, not unreasonably.

After a sales meeting, he told her, he had gone out to have a few drinks with one of his old friends and they got drunk. He was so drunk, in fact, that he could not navigate home, so he'd slept on his friend's couch. He had not telephoned because he knew she was tired and didn't want to awaken her.

"I told him I didn't believe him," Pam chirped, "but he didn't want to talk about it anymore."

Later in the day, she added, he called her at work and repeated the same story, and again she told him that she thought he was lying. Again he denied it. Later, when she persisted in learning more details, Gregg brushed her off, saying that she did not want to know the truth.

"Then," she said, "I *knew* he was lying."

She kept after him to tell her what had happened, and he confessed that he had spent the night with another woman.

"I was mad," she said. "We argued about it. He said he had been drinking and he didn't even remember. I said that was a poor excuse. I was devastated. I was very hurt. I didn't talk to him for about a day."

"How did it make you feel?" prompted Twomey.

"I didn't feel as important anymore," Pam said softly. "Obviously it affected my trust."

She tried to put it out of her mind, she said, but she could not. And then, three days before Christmas, another incident occurred.

She and Gregg had been to a holiday party, she said, along with Gregg's parents, William and Judith, and Gregg had too much to drink. His parents drove them home, and everything seemed all right. But once they got inside the apartment, they began arguing.

"Gregg wasn't making any sense," Pam said, "so I started getting ready for bed."

She put on a sweatshirt and sweatpants and was about to crawl beneath the covers when the argument flared up again. She was so angry with Gregg because of his behavior, she said, that she told him she was leaving and started for the door. He reached for her in an attempt to stop her, and when he did the side of his hand grazed her jaw.

"He didn't mean to hit me," she said sadly, adding that Gregg had never beaten her and that she had never told anyone, especially Bill Flynn, that he had.

She was so angry, she said, that she stomped out the door and slammed it behind her, only to realize that she didn't have any keys. Still angry, she walked, apparently barefoot and without a coat, to Gregg's parents' house about a block away.

Crying and upset, she explained to her husband's parents that they had had a fight and she had accidentally locked herself out. Gregg's father went to his son's condo and banged on the door, but Gregg did not answer. He tried telephoning, but Gregg let it ring.

"We found out later that Gregg had passed out," she said.

When he sobered up and she told him what had happened, he was extremely contrite.

Deviating momentarily from the story of her marriage, Pam then explained how she had become involved with the teenagers at Winnacunnet High, how she had taken the job with the school district—essentially a public relations job—and volunteered to help in Project Self-Esteem. It was through the program, she confirmed, that she met Cecelia, Bill, and J.R.

Cecelia was gregarious and very interested in

Pam's job. She wanted to be a journalist, Pam explained, and her job seemed an attractive alternative.

She was aware of who Pete Randall was, she said, realizing that he was a friend of Bill's, but as well as she could remember, she had only two conversations with him.

"Actually," she corrected herself, "I don't know if I ever had a conversation directly with him. He was just part of a group involved in a general conversation."

However, she did not deny that she was attracted to Bill almost from the beginning.

"I thought he was a good kid," she said. "He was easy to talk to, friendly. He liked some of the same music I liked. He played the guitar."

But, she implied, had it not been for a flier that arrived in the mail announcing the orange juice commercial contest, the relationship with Bill might have ended right there.

When Cecelia, with whom Pam had become quite friendly, saw the flier she got excited about the idea and pressed Pam to get involved. Pam agreed to go along and told Cecelia to begin getting a crew together to work on the project. Eventually the crew shook down to Pam, Cecelia, Tracy Collins, Rachel Emond, and Bill.

"We did all our own audio and video," Pam said proudly. "We wrote our own song."

As the work on the commercial progressed, so did the relationship with Bill. Pam said she was aware that Bill had a crush on her because she had been told so by Cecelia.

"And," she admitted, "I had begun to like him."

Nevertheless, she added, she told him that although she liked him, she was married and therefore she was not interested in having a relationship with him.

"I didn't set out to have an affair with him," she said, lowering her voice modestly, "but I did."

It began, she said, one day when she was at his house and they were working on the commercial. They were in his room, she added, with the door closed, when he leaned over and kissed her.

She was so confused, she said, that she immediately went home. "I really didn't want to have an affair, and I was trying to fight my feelings."

It was, she admitted, an uphill battle—one she subsequently lost. Several weeks later, on March 24, she gave up the fight.

Gregg was in Atlantic City on business, she recalled, and Cecelia was staying at her house while her husband was gone. Bill asked if he could come over as well, and she consented.

"I *wanted* him to come over," she added.

At that point Twomey interrupted her narrative with a question. When Bill came over, he asked, did she expect to have sex with him?

"Yes," Pam replied quietly.

"And *did* you have sex with him?"

"Yes."

He wanted to know if they had watched the movie *9 1/2 Weeks* and if afterward she had made love to him.

"Yes," she responded.

"Did you do that thing with the ice cubes?"

"No," she said emphatically, that was a figment of Bill's imagination. "I think he's having a problem remembering where reality began and the movie stopped."

At this stage her testimony roughly paralleled that of the earlier witnesses, especially Bill's and Cecelia's, but it differed in several major respects. For one thing, she had altered the beginning of the affair by some six weeks. It was Bill's recollection that they watched *9 1/2 Weeks* in mid-February, maybe on the day after Valentine's. Pam said it was March 24. Bill said she initiated the physical contact by inviting him to kiss her when they were at his house; she said it was Bill's move.

Bill said he distinctly remembered getting a glass of ice cubes and using them in their lovemaking, as had been portrayed in the movie. Cecelia also said she recalled Bill coming downstairs, getting the cubes, and returning to the bedroom. Pam said the incident never occurred.

But those were not the only instances where the testimony differed. There were more to come.

Regarding the photos that Bill had of Pam in her bikini, the ones that he said she had given him even before the affair began, Pam claimed that she had *not* offered them to Bill and she did not know how he got them.

And as far as the notes they were supposed to have exchanged, she admitted writing a few, some of which may have been considered by some to be sexually explicit.

And as far as their affair went, Pam said, it was begun impulsively and quickly terminated.

"I *liked* Bill," she testified, "but I *loved* Gregg."

Possibly, she confessed, she had loved Bill too at one point, but that had only fed her confusion and pained her conscience.

Twomey again interrupted. "Did you ever tell your husband about this?" he asked.

Pam sighed. "Yes," she said, "I did." Then she launched into a detailed version of what had happened when Gregg discovered he had been cuckolded.

26

IT WAS ON APRIL 27, she remembered, the Friday before he was murdered.

"There had been quite a few occasions when I wanted to tell him, but I had not," Pam recalled.

On that day she had left work early so she would have some more time with Gregg, so she could confess to him what had been going on in her life. Just two days earlier Bill had spent the night at the condo when Gregg had been out of town, and it had been an incredibly domestic evening. Pam had cooked dinner and Bill had cleared the table, done the dishes, and carried out the trash, taking the garbage down the cellar stairs and out through the outside door called the bulkhead, the same door Bill would later use to enter the condo when he came to kill Gregg.

After dinner, Pam said, they went upstairs, climbed into her marital bed, and made love. The next day she had told Bill the affair was ended, that they could be friends but no longer lovers. After that she wanted to make peace with Gregg and see if they could resolve their problems.

That Friday evening she sat quietly with Gregg, she said, letting him unwind and tell her about his trip. One night after their series of business meetings, Gregg told her, some of the men had brought a hooker into the hotel and took turns using her services.

This, Pam figured, was the opening she had been waiting for. Did *he*, she asked, wait his turn in line? Gregg was shocked. No, he replied, he would *never* do that.

Never? Pam shot back. Well, how about the night in December when he had not come home?

Gregg got angry and asked Pam if she was going to keep bringing up his one previous infidelity.

"I asked him how he would have felt if I had done something like that," Pam said, "and he answered by saying that he wouldn't be too happy, but he wouldn't throw it in my face for the rest of his life. So I told him about my affair," she said, pausing dramatically. "He wasn't happy. He said he couldn't believe I would do that."

She said she then told him that the affair was over and that she wanted to make their marriage work. She did not tell him Bill's name or explain their connection, she added.

Again Twomey interrupted, asking her if she

had made any previous attempts to break off the relationship with Bill before the final one.

"Yes," she replied contritely. "I told him I didn't feel right about the relationship. I told him I loved Gregg, that I didn't want a divorce."

Anxious to insert material that he hoped would demolish the prosecution witnesses' claims that Pam had said she could not get a divorce because Gregg would take everything, Twomey asked her what the two of them had owned jointly.

Brightening, Pam related that the two of them owned the furniture, and their bank accounts were in both their names. Gregg owned his own car, she said, and she, hers. The dog technically was hers because it had been a graduation present from Gregg. "I knew he had some life insurance," she added, "but I didn't know how much."

Twomey wanted to know how Bill had responded when she told him that the affair was over.

He started to cry, she said. He said he couldn't live without her, that he was going to kill himself. She said that she responded by telling him they could still be friends, but that she loved Gregg and she felt guilty about her relationship with him. As a consequence, she had decided to break off the affair, confess to Gregg, and beg his forgiveness.

When she said they could still be friends, Bill stopped sobbing and seemed to cheer up. She said she told him that it would be better if he did not come over to the media center anymore, but she relented when he said that he did not want to stop seeing her altogether.

Bouncing to another subject, Twomey asked Pam if she had ever let Bill use her car.

Yes, she said, twice. But both times, she added, she made sure that there was someone else driving because Bill did not yet have his driver's license, although he had recently become old enough to apply.

When was it, Twomey asked, that Bill had asked to use her CRX?

The most recent time, she remembered, was late in April. Bill called her one afternoon and asked if he and J.R. could use her car to go to Haverhill. At first she told him no, but he called back a little later and she agreed. She had a meeting to attend that evening, she pointed out, so she would not need the car back until well after dark, but she had to have it back in time to go home. There was one more condition: J.R. had to be the driver because she didn't want anyone who did not have a license driving her car. That would be illegal.

She agreed to leave the keys in the car so Bill and J.R. could pick it up. After that she thought no more about it until her meeting was over and she got ready to leave, only to find that her car had not yet been returned. So she had to wait. She was afraid that others in the building, seeing her sitting in her office, would question her about her car and who had it. Since she was not anxious for it to be known that she had let a student named Bill Flynn use it, she turned off the lights in her office and waited in the dark for Bill and J.R. to return. But when her car came back, it was not J.R. who was with Bill, but another teenager whom she had never met. His name was Raymond Fowler.

"I asked Bill, 'Who is this?' and he said, 'This is Raymond. You remember Raymond, don't you?' And I said, 'No.'"

She asked Bill if Raymond had a license and he said yes, so she felt a little better. She was still angry, she remembered, because Bill had told her that he and J.R. would be using the car, not someone she had never even met. In any case, she drove Raymond home and then took Bill to his house. On the drive, she said, she had the car radio playing loudly and she was not eager to engage in conversation, mainly because she was still angry that Bill had lied to her about who would be with him in the car. After she dropped them off and headed home, she said, she pushed the incident out of her mind.

In an attempt to keep her from wandering too far afield, Twomey stopped her and asked how many times Bill had visited her condo in Derry.

Pam hardly had to think about it. "Three times," she replied quickly. Once when they were working on the orange juice commercial; again when they watched *9 1/2 Weeks*; and a third time when she cooked dinner for the two of them and Bill spent the night.

"And did you ever give Bill money to buy bullets to kill Gregg?" Twomey asked.

Absolutely not, Pam replied.

With the background set, Twomey asked her to describe what happened on the day Gregg was murdered.

She took a deep breath and launched into her narrative.

On the morning of Tuesday, May 1, 1990, she slept late.

Knowing she had an important meeting to attend that night, one in which school board members would be talking about three issues close to her heart—her salary, the proposed remodeling of the media center, and the possibility she might be allowed to teach a course in the high school the next fall—she planned to go into the office late and work straight through until the session began.

But when she got there she remembered that it was Secretary's Week and she and the other department heads in the building planned to take the secretaries to lunch in Portsmouth, a short drive up the coast. They left Hampton at about eleven-thirty, she said, and did not get back until two-thirty. By the time they returned, school was out and all the students had left for the day.

Twomey nodded encouragingly as she talked.

By mentioning the time she returned, he hoped she would throw doubt on Cecelia's claim that Pam had told her in the afternoon that Gregg would be murdered that evening. If Pam did not get back to Hampton until after Cecelia had already gone home, she could not possibly have told her, therefore Cecelia must have been lying.

It seemed that she had no sooner gotten back from Portsmouth, Pam recalled, than Bill called and asked her if she would drive him and J.R. to Haverhill so J.R. could pick up his grandmother's car.

"I said no," Pam claimed. "I said I had been gone all day and I wanted to get to work."

About an hour or an hour and a half later, Bill called back and asked her again. He sounded so pitiful, she recalled, that she agreed. But when she got to J.R.'s house to pick up Bill and J.R., Pete was there as well. He asked if he could go along so he could keep J.R. company on the trip back. Pam said she was not anxious to drive back alone, either, so she said okay.

Because J.R. asked, she let him drive while she and Bill climbed in the back. On the drive, they chatted about motorcycles and about her car.

"Did you discuss a plan to murder your husband?" Twomey asked.

"No," Pam said simply, although she admitted that she had to ask J.R. to slow down at least once. "I told him I didn't want to get a ticket because we had four people in my car, which was a two-seater, and I believe that's against the law."

Maggiotto, who had been listening attentively to Pam's testimony, rolled his eyes in disbelief and slowly shook his head.

"What happened next?" prompted Twomey.

They dropped off Pete and J.R., she said, then she and Bill returned to Seabrook. She left Bill at J.R.'s house, and she went back to the office. Digging in at her desk, she worked straight through until just before her meeting was to start. She was interrupted when Cecelia dropped by, along with her boyfriend, Michael Welch. They stayed about three minutes, she recalled, and left to go to dinner. When they left, she went to her meeting. Afterward, since it was dark, her secretary's husband, who was a member of the school board, walked her to her car, as was customary, and she drove home to Derry.

This was the point that Twomey had been waiting patiently for her to reach. It was now, if at all, that her credibility would be cemented. To overcome the damage that previous testimony had done, particularly Bill's, Pam would have to be believable on this issue or her case would go down the tubes. And to establish herself, she had to let loose a little; she had to show some emotion and prove that she was not the "Ice Princess" the media had dubbed her.

Gallantly she rose to the occasion.

27

THAT'S ODD, Pam remembered thinking as she pulled up to her condo, the outside lights are not on.

Gregg usually turned those on first thing so she would not have to go to the door in the dark. But they were dark, and she recalled feeling apprehensive because she was sure that Gregg had beaten her home by a wide margin. Shrugging off the premonition that something was wrong, she parked her car, walked to the door, and turned her key in the lock. Reaching in, she flipped on the foyer lights and took a single step inside. Then she stopped in her tracks. Stretched out on the floor, facedown, was Gregg, his head in a pool of blood.

"This all happened in a matter of not even a second, I think," she said. "I remember seeing him and the candlestick and the pillow."

Moisture started building in her eyes, and her lips quivered. It was the first sign of any strong emotion that court watchers had seen in her since the trial began.

"The first thing I thought was to go get help." But she hesitated slightly. "I said Gregg's name. He didn't answer me, so I ran out."

"Did you know he was dead then?" Twomey asked gently.

"No," she said, threatening to cry, "I thought maybe somebody else was in the house."

She then described a frantic attempt to find aid. "No one would help me," she said. "I ran next door. I was ringing the doorbell. I was screaming 'Call the police!' but they didn't come fast enough. So I ran to the next house and started banging on it. By that time a girl was already coming down the stairs because I guess she heard me screaming. She asked me what was wrong.

"Apparently someone had already called 911. I remember I went back outside, and all kinds of cars and people had come. I was crying. I said, 'Call Gregg's parents,' and I gave them the phone number."

In just a few minutes, she said, Gregg's mother and father arrived, along with one of Gregg's brothers. They kept asking her, she recalled tearfully, where Gregg was and what was the matter. Gregg's mother tried to go into the condo, but the police stopped her.

"Everyone was screaming at me and I was crying," she said. "I was on my knees on the ground. Then an ambulance came and two men went inside."

She remembered Gregg's brother begging

224

them to help Gregg, but it seemed as if no one was doing anything.

Pam's demeanor, as she related the events of the night of May 1, was calm, but her face was cloudy. At this point she began to choke up.

"They said," she said, swallowing hard, "that he was dead."

The next thing she remembered was being at the Smarts' house. The next few hours went by in a fog, and at about two A.M. she went to the Derry police station to tell her story. Some two hours later she finished, got in her car, and drove to her parents' house in Canobie Lake. They stayed up all night talking about the incident.

Even then, she claimed, the police were refusing to give her any information. At first she was under the impression that Gregg had been killed by a blow to the head with the candlestick she had seen on the floor. She did not know until much later that he had been shot. She found that out, she said, by hearing it on a news report on her car radio. From the very beginning, she said, she was shut out of the investigation, and the only way she could discover what was going on was from news reports.

The next major development occurred about five weeks later, she said. On Sunday, June 10, Bill had come to visit her at her new condo in Hampton, a short stroll away from Winnacunnet High. They went to a movie, then came home and watched a couple more on videotape. Since it was so late, Bill asked if he could stay overnight. At this time they were nothing more than friends, she claimed, and when he asked she consented. She said she made him a bed on the couch and she went upstairs to bed.

The next morning she was in the shower when the doorbell rang. Letting Bill answer it, she finished her shower, got dressed, and went downstairs. What she found was Bill talking excitedly to J.R. and Pete.

When she asked what was going on, Bill told her that Pete had gotten into a fight with another youth named Ralph Welch because Ralph was saying some things about Pete that were not true. It was nothing for her to worry about, Bill suggested, and she probably should just go back upstairs. Later, when she came down again, she found Pete and J.R. still there.

"They used the phone a few times," she recalled, "but I don't know who they called."

Sometime later J.R.'s mother called and said there was a family emergency and he needed to come home. Bill decided to go with him and Pete. But since J.R. and Pete had come on a motorbike and only two could ride on it, they asked Pam if she would drive them to J.R.'s. She agreed.

After dropping J.R. at his house and Pete and Bill at a small store nearby, she went shopping and planned to go home from there. As she was driving home, though, she saw Bill, Pete, and J.R. walking down the road. She stopped and offered them a ride.

When she asked J.R. and Pete when they were

going to take the motorbike that was still in her garage, they said they would take it then. So they returned to her condo, got on the bike, and roared off. Bill told her he was leaving as well, and the last she saw of him, until he appeared in court, he was walking away toward Winnacunnet High.

That evening, several hours after Bill left, Pam was alone in her condo when her doorbell rang. It was Cecelia and her boyfriend, Michael Welch.

They came in, she recalled, and they started talking. After a few minutes, Cecelia asked if she could stay with her that night, and she said yes. Michael decided to go home, Pam said, so she drove Cecelia to her house so she could pick up some fresh clothes for school the next day.

On the way back, with Cecelia at the wheel (she had no driver's license, but that was all right, Pam said, because she was in the car with her and Cecelia was approaching the age where she could take the test and get her license), they were pulled over by a mob of police.

"They were not at all friendly," Pam recalled. "They surrounded the car and put these big spotlights on us and told us not to move a muscle."

Her dog, Halen, was in the car, Pam said, and he became frightened by all the activity. When she grabbed for him to calm him down, the police apparently thought she was reaching for a weapon and they reacted with surprising abruptness. One of the officers glared at her and ordered her not to move again. A few seconds later, a female officer came up to the car and asked Cecelia for her driver's license and registration.

"I was trying to explain, but the woman was so mean," Pam said. "She was screaming. I was really nervous. It was very intimidating."

She said soon afterward she heard a voice over the police radio instructing the officers on the scene to let them go with the explanation that they had made a mistake and pulled over the wrong car, which was exactly what the female officer told her seconds later.

"I'm not that stupid," Pam said she told them.

She was listening to the eleven o'clock news the next night, Monday, when she heard that three juveniles had been arrested in connection with the murder of Gregory Smart of Derry.

"I was upset," she said. "First of all, someone was arrested in connection with my husband's death and I didn't know anything of it. And second, I had to find out about it from the news. The news report said the arrests were in Seabrook, so I didn't know if it was someone who was going to come after me."

Never suspecting, she said, that the three youths who had been arrested were Bill, Pete, and J.R., she began making a series of telephone calls to see what she could find out.

First she called her secretary, whose husband was a member of the school board, but that was a dead end. She called the Derry police but was told that no one from the detective division was working that late. Early the next morning she tried to call Bill and then Cecelia to see if they knew anything.

When she called Bill's house, his mother answered and Pam identified herself. What Bill's mother told her left her numb, Pam said. Mrs. Flynn reported that Bill, J.R., and Pete had been arrested, Bill for first-degree murder and the other two as accomplices.

"My reaction was total shock and disbelief," she testified. "I could not believe Bill could be arrested. And then I thought, Oh, my God, they've found out about the affair and they've arrested the wrong person."

Pam said Bill's mother told her they had evidence linking him to the crime, but she could not tell her what kind of evidence it was. Then, according to Pam, she said something very strange.

"She told me," Pam recalled, "that I had better get a lawyer. When I said why, she said I just had better do it."

Really upset by that time, Pam said, she drove to her parents' house and tried again to contact the Derry police. Again, according to her, they stonewalled her.

"They told me the same thing they had been telling me throughout the investigation. They said they couldn't tell me anything. And now, because juveniles were involved, they said they couldn't tell me anything because the suspects were juveniles."

Twomey asked her how she had felt about the developments.

"I had a very hard time believing Bill had committed this crime," she said, adding that Gregg's murder was something she had been thinking about all the time. "Everyone was asking me for the answers, and I was asking everyone else. I felt like I was nothing. I felt like I was a reporter seeking information for no other reason than to report it to the rest of the world. I did not feel like the victim's wife. I'd turn on the TV every night to find out what was going on in my life. That's how bad it was."

In desperation, she said, she turned to two sources: Cecelia and the media.

Almost through with his questions, Twomey asked Pam to tell the court about the incidents leading up to the recordings that Cecelia had made of their conversations.

Pam shrugged. Cecelia, she said, was constantly calling her in the hours after Bill, J.R., and Pete were arrested.

"She was very nervous," Pam recalled. "Very excited; very worried. I got to wondering what she was so worried about."

Finally, she said, she determined that Cecelia knew more than what she had been telling her. For one thing, Cecelia knew about her affair with

Bill, but Pam reckoned her knowledge included more than that.

"My only sources of information were Cecelia and the news," Pam contended. "I was totally obsessed with finding out who murdered my husband. So I figured if she knew more about the murder, she would tell me if I acted like *I* knew more about it. I thought I'd play a game with her and pretend I knew more about the murder."

What was the point? Twomey prompted.

"To get information." Pam responded quickly. "All the information I was getting indicated the kids were guilty, but I didn't want to believe it. In my heart I didn't want to believe that someone I knew had done this. I was totally obsessed with learning what had happened. I used to sit in bed every single night and wonder what happened to Gregg. I didn't care about anything else."

To get information, she insisted in what would be a major plank in her defense, she decided to lead Cecelia along, pretending to know more than she did so Cecelia would tell her what *she* knew, thereby helping Pam solve the mystery of her own husband's murder. That was why, she would tell Maggiotto a few minutes later, she sounded so well informed about the crime on the tapes with Cecelia: she was pretending in order to develop evidence. The prosecutor didn't believe it for a second. And neither would the jury.

28

By THE TIME the prosecution got its shot at
Pam, Paul Maggiotto was practically dancing on
the tabletop, as anxious to join the battle as a
contender in the first round of a title bout.

Working up to the murder, Maggiotto first
went after Pam because of her silence about her
affair with Bill. If, as she had said, she wanted
to see her husband's murder solved, why had she
not shared with investigators information that
may have helped them close the case? Heark-
ening back to her testimony of an hour or so pre-
viously, when she'd said that when she first
heard about Bill's arrest her initial thought had
been that they had found out about the affair
and had arrested the wrong person, he asked her
why she had not told investigators about the
affair then.

"Because I thought if the police knew I had an
affair with Bill, they would automatically con-
clude that I was involved in the murder," she
replied, as cool as whipped cream.

"So rather than get the possibly wrong person
off, you kept quiet, is that right?"

When she answered in the affirmative, Maggiotto asked if that had been a conscious decision on her part, a judgment that could have had disastrous results for her young lover if indeed he had been innocent.

Well, yes, she conceded, volunteering that another reason she'd kept mum about the affair was that the police never asked her.

Maggiotto threw his hands in the air. "Oh," he said with elaborate sarcasm, "they never asked you! If they would have asked you, you would have told them, right?"

Unflustered, Pam replied: "I can't speculate on that because I don't know. If I had been sitting in a room full of police, I might have told them."

It was a theme Maggiotto would return to several times before the confrontation was over: repeatedly he asked her why she had not said such-and-such in a particular situation, and she replied repeatedly that no one had asked her. Each time the scene repeated itself, the prosecutor seemed to get more frustrated and Pam more obstinate.

Later in his cross-examination, when he ran into the same intransigence again, he growled that with Pam truth appeared to be relative to the situation she found herself in. "Truth to you depends on what is at stake. Is that right?"

"No, not at all," she said defensively.

But, he continued, you have said that if they don't ask you a specific question, you don't give them an answer. "If they don't ring the bell or pull the string, no one is ever going to know about it, correct?"

"I guess not," she admitted grudgingly.

In essence, Maggiotto pointed out, her contention was that she was now admitting an affair with Bill Flynn but was denying any connection with Gregg's murder.

Pam bobbed her head, as if Maggiotto had just made the most rational statement in the world. "Yes!" she said.

But, the prosecutor shot back, isn't that *exactly* what she told Cecelia she would do during one of their tape-recorded conversations?

Without batting an eye, Pam admitted that also was correct.

"Well, which was more important to you?" he asked. "Finding the killer of your husband or keeping the affair quiet?"

"Finding the killer of my husband," she replied, adding that a week after the murder she had become somewhat suspicious of Bill and had confronted him. "I asked him, 'You didn't have anything to do with this, did you?' and he said no."

Naturally, Maggiotto said, she had passed on that tidbit to the police.

"No," she said.

In that case, he pursued, she'd probably said something to William and Judith Smart.

"No," Pam said.

Well, how about her family?

"No," she said again.

Had she mentioned to *anyone*, he asked, the fact that, according to her, she had broken off her relationship with her lover just a few days before her husband was murdered? "Did you say to anyone, 'Hey, a week before Gregg was murdered I broke up with a kid and he might have had something to do with it?'"

She admitted she had not.

Feigning amazement, he asked her why not.

Because, she answered, at the time it looked as though Gregg had been killed in a botched burglary and had not been a victim of a premeditated murder. The implication was she was not about to reveal the affair unless she was backed into a corner and there was no other possible avenue of escape, such as a trial.

No matter which angle Maggiotto approached Pam from on the subject of the affair, she seemed always to dance away before he could land a telling blow. The more excited he got in his pursuit, the calmer she seemed to become and the more ostensibly cooperative. Unlike other witnesses in the case who were content to answer as many questions as possible with a simple yes or no, Pam seemed to enjoy enlarging upon her answers and going beyond the question that was asked her. Several times she anticipated what Maggiotto was leading up to and answered his questions before he could ask them, a ploy that irritated the prosecutor immensely because it threw his timing off. If he was going to catch Pam in a trap of her own making, he had to do it methodically. And he was not going to get there unless he could verbally block off her escape route.

Once, when he was asking her a series of questions leading up to a specific point, she blurted out a response that was not the one he was hoping to elicit from her. "If there's anything else you want to tell the jury voluntarily before I've asked it," he said tightly, "go right ahead."

"Nope," she replied calmly, looking as if she wanted to smile.

In one sense Mark Sisti had been operating at a disadvantage because the witnesses he cross-examined were teenagers and he had to be careful about how aggressively he attacked them. If he appeared to be browbeating or harassing them unnecessarily, there could have been a backlash among the jurors no matter how justified he may have been in using whatever means he could to pry admissions from them.

Maggiotto, on the other hand, was under no such constraints. Thanks in large part to her own attitude, as well as to the fact that there had been a large amount of damaging testimony against her, Pam was fair game. The prosecutor was free to go after her as pugnaciously as he wanted with only Judge Gray to rein him in.

At several points during Maggiotto's questioning, Twomey bounced to his feet and complained to the judge that the prosecutor was badgering the witness. Gray, as many judges would do under similar circumstances, refused to order Maggiotto to restrain himself. Cross-examination is a dog-eat-dog process, and courts generally allow a good deal of latitude in the direction of combative questioning.

Pam's statements about her affair with Bill differed considerably from his, not only in the length of time the romance lasted, but in its intensity as well. Take the issue of sex, for example.

When Bill was on the stand, he swore that he and Pam used every opportunity they could to copulate, consummating their love in the backseat of her car, on the beach, on *his* bed, on *her* bed, on the bed in J.R.'s grandmother's camper, on the floor, and on the ground. Sometimes, he said, they made love as many as seven times in an afternoon. But when Maggiotto asked Pam about their lovemaking arrangements, she said they had sex exactly three times: twice in her condo and once in Bill's bedroom. Even allowing for a large amount of male teenage braggadocio, half the people in the courtroom raised their eyebrows when Pam insisted she was being accurate.

Then there was the issue of the pictures of her in her bikini, pictures she swore she never gave to him.

What was the prosecutor so upset about? she wanted to know. The pictures were no big deal.

Maggiotto strolled over to the exhibit clerk and retrieved them. Then he handed them to Pam and invited her to describe them.

"It's just a couple of people in bathing suits standing around posing," she said.

"*Standing* around?" he asked, pointing out that for the most part she hardly was standing. "Maybe kneeling on a bed?" he suggested. "Posing, shall we say, provocatively?"

"Umm, maybe," Pam conceded. "I suppose you could call the poses provocative." But only, she added, someone whose mind was in the gutter.

"Your testimony is you never gave these pictures to Bill Flynn, right?"

"Right!" she said.

Well, he asked, switching subjects, how about the single note in Pam's handwriting that had been recovered, apparently a love note?

Pam looked as if she wanted to smile again. That was no love note, she contended, it was simply the lyrics of a song that she had copied down because she liked the way the words sounded. The song, "First Love" by the heavy metal religious group Stryker, was about God, she said smugly, and had nothing to do with illicit romance or sex.

What about the other notes that she had admitted writing? Maggiotto asked. By her own description some of them were fairly racy.

Well, she responded, that fell into the same category as the pictures: whether they were suggestive depended on the attitude of the observer.

"Were they sexually explicit?" he asked.

"I don't remember specific lines," she said evasively, "but, yes, there was talk about sex, but it depends on what you consider sexually explicit. Maybe you consider those photos sexually explicit, but I don't."

Did the notes contain graphic sexual descriptions?

"Not that I remember," she said.

Finally there was the seduction night issue.

Tell me about *Nine and a Half Weeks*, he invited.

"I guess it has sex in it," she said. "I don't remember."

How about the dance? Maggiotto asked. Did you dance for Bill as Kim Basinger had done in the movie?

Part of what Bill had said about that is true, she conceded. "There was a negligee involved, but there was no dance."

Maggiotto shook his head. First she denied there were any ice cubes. Then she denied there was any dance. In a way, he was surprised that she had even admitted watching the movie.

"When you broke up with him for final time, when was it?" Maggiotto continued doggedly.

"A Wednesday or a Thursday," she replied, referring to the week prior to the one in which Gregg was murdered.

"So, on Tuesday night everything was peachy keen. You didn't tell him Tuesday night. When he left your house, he left thinking everything was okay?"

"I suppose," she answered coolly.

"Yet," Maggiotto asked, raising his voice, "you want this jury to understand that Bill Flynn decided to kill your husband because you broke up with him."

"I want this jury to understand the truth."

"That's what you're claiming the truth is?"

She skipped away, evading the question. "I don't know why Bill Flynn killed Gregg," she said. "I can just come here and give my testimony."

Maggiotto would not let it go. "Why do you *think* he did it?"

"Probably because he thought we could be together," she replied.

It was not much, but it was an admission of sorts. After several hours of sparring, the prosecutor was the one expending all the energy. He looked frazzled and frustrated; she looked calm and cool. But the fight had just begun.

Tell me about Cecelia, the prosecutor urged, hoping she would open up.

Pam didn't hesitate. "I think she has a tendency to want to be the star," she said. "She's a good person, though."

Over the months, she related, they became friends, and like most friends, they had occasional disagreements.

"When we got into fights it was usually because she was jealous of other people being around me," Pam said. At times like that she would say things to hurt her. "Things like I looked fat. Stupid things."

This was not the way Maggiotto wanted it to go. Pam had succeeded in slipping in an implication that Cecelia may have been motivated by jealousy in an attempt to frame Pam.

"When did she start talking to you about the case?" Maggiotto asked.

Pam said she started getting suspicious the day after Bill, Pete, and J.R. were arrested. It was something in Cecelia's tone of voice that alerted her, she said, a note of excitement, or nervousness, or worry.

Maggiotto stopped her, claiming what she was saying did not make sense. If she was afraid of her telephone being tapped, as she had testified she was, why did she continue to talk to Cecelia about the murder over the telephone?

In the July 13 conversation, Pam said, she told Cecelia that she knew about the murder before it happened to see what she would say. And Cecelia responded that Bill had never told her (Cecelia) that she (Pam) knew. Pam claimed that was a revelation, confirmation of her suspicion that Cecelia knew more than she was admitting to. As a result, she said, she decided to increase her efforts to dig out what Cecelia was keeping hidden.

"So what you're saying is it was just a trick to try to get more information from Cecelia?" Maggiotto asked.

"Right," Pam confirmed.

241

"So she confirms what you want her to say," Maggiotto conceded for argument's sake. "Now tell the jury why you didn't go to the police with that information."

Because, Pam said, in the same conversation Cecelia had told her that there had been a previous attempt on Gregg's life and that was something she was not yet ready to believe. She needed more time to work that out.

"It was the first I had heard of it," she said. "Also, if I had told the police what I knew, then they would have found out about the affair."

She didn't want that, she added. Plus she didn't feel obligated to share her knowledge with the police because they weren't telling *her* anything.

"I was afraid that if I gave them information, they would run with it and I'd be back at square one and not know anything."

"In other words," Maggiotto said, "you were going to do your own little investigation?"

"Yes," Pam admitted. "I was not acting rationally at all. My husband was murdered."

"And the last thing you want to do," he snapped sarcastically, "is give the police some good information to help them solve the murder."

"No," she replied, seemingly wounded.

"Oh, you wanted to tell them?" he asked, assuming her answer would be no.

"I was confused," she said, wiggling away.

29

ON THE WITNESS STAND, however, Pam seemed anything but confused. Cool, calculating, focused, and determined, perhaps, with more than a tad of arrogance thrown in. But she was hardly baffled.

On Tuesday, her second day on the stand, wearing a green suit with a black velvet collar and her traditional bow, she seemed even more entrenched than she had the previous day. Although he was logging seventy-five working hours a week during the trial, Maggiotto also appeared refreshed when he and Pam squared off anew.

Jumping immediately back into the debate on why she was so tormented with the need to cover up her affair with Bill, Maggiotto suggested that it could have been both a personal and professional disaster for Pam if it became known that she had been carrying on covertly with a fifteen-year-old male, and that may have been her real motive.

"But there would be less chance of the affair becoming public if Gregg were dead, wouldn't it?" he asked.

"I'm admitting the affair because it's the truth," she replied, evading the question entirely.

Recognizing a stonewall when he saw one, the prosecutor skipped ahead, asking Pam what she possibly could have expected to learn from Cecelia even if her plan to pry out information had been successful. "What did she tell you that you didn't know?"

Now *that* was a question that Pam was eager to address.

She told her, Pam answered promptly, that there had been a prior attempt on Gregg's life; that Cecelia had gone with Bill to Papa Gino's to look for a gun; that Raymond was with Bill the first time he went ostensibly to kill Gregg; and that they had taken her car on the unproductive journey—all things she claimed she had not been aware of. Also, she added after pausing for breath, she had learned from Cecelia that Bill had been the murderer, that Pete and J.R. were with him, and that they had dropped gloves at the scene.

"Where was Cecelia getting all this information?" Maggiotto asked skeptically, hoping Pam would work herself into a position from which she could not extricate herself.

"I assume that Bill had told her," Pam replied.

That was a bit too much for the prosecutor. Although both Bill and Cecelia had testified that they knew each other, the relationship had not been exactly a confidence-sharing one. Plus, the relationship between Pam and Cecelia *had* been one of shared confidences, and it hardly seemed plausible to him, he said, that Cecelia would have waited until almost six weeks after the murder, two days after Pete, J.R., and Bill were arrested, to mention these details to her.

"No," Pam answered coolly, "we talked about the murder every day."

"But she never said, 'Hey, your husband's dead and maybe I can help you find out who killed him?'" Maggiotto asked, a touch of incredulity in his voice. "You're saying that Cecelia intentionally withheld information from you about the murder of your husband?"

"Yes," Pam answered, as if it were the most reasonable question in the world. "That was probably because she had some involvement herself. At least she had some knowledge of it. My idea is she had her own involvement through helping secure a firearm, so she was protecting herself."

Pam was proving as hard to grasp as a wet bar of soap. But, Maggiotto reminded himself, every time she turned slippery, a little more of her personality was exposed to the jury. Even if it didn't seem he was making much progress in getting any significant answers from her, it was a performance the jury would remember later. He hoped.

"Why," he asked, going back to another old theme, "did you try to talk her out of going to the police?"

Because, Pam replied, if Cecelia had opened up to investigators, she also would have told them that she (Pam) had claimed to know about the murder in advance. "I didn't want her to do that. So I automatically panicked. I was scared. I had heard rumors that I was going to be arrested, and I was afraid."

"And you thought the best way to deal with that," Maggiotto asked sarcastically, "is not that honesty is the best policy. You decided not to go to the police and let them sort it out, but to withhold information and start playing mind games with Cecelia?"

Pam nodded in agreement. At the time, she said, that seemed like the wisest move.

But, Maggiotto plowed ahead, if she knew that Cecelia had valuable information, she could have encouraged the teenager to take a lie detector test instead of discouraging her as enthusiastically as she had. That way, at least, police may have been able to solve the murder.

"Yeah," said Pam, "and she also would be on the lie detector talking about my affair and how I knew about Gregg's murder beforehand. I wanted to solve it in my own mind, in my own way, first."

Maggiotto grimaced. "Then what were you going to do?" he demanded. "Make a citizen's arrest?"

"No," Pam answered with a straight face. "At some point obviously I would have gone to the police with it."

No matter how hard he hammered, Maggiotto was unable to shake Pam's testimony. Whatever approach he tried, she countered successfully. When he kept insisting that her refusal to go to the police was irrational as well as personally dangerous, she kept replying that she could not do that until she had wrung as much information as she could out of Cecelia. Once she had lied to Cecelia about knowing about the murder in advance, she could not back away until she had the entire story. Otherwise Cecelia would simply have passed on to the police that information as well as what she knew about Pam's affair with Bill.

"I want this jury to believe the truth," Pam said. "I kept things from the police. I was trying to hide an affair. But I was twenty-two years old and I made the wrong decisions."

As the cross-examination continued, Pam's testimony changed very subtly. Although she had admitted many times that she had untruthfully told Cecelia that she had known about the plan to kill Gregg, she then added a new wrinkle: she said she told Cecelia that *Bill* knew that she knew.

Thinking he may have found a weak spot he could exploit, Maggiotto pounced.

Wasn't that inconsistent with what she had been saying all along? he asked.

Not at all, she replied breezily. One statement followed the other. If *she* knew about it, it was only natural that her *lover* would know that she knew.

Wheels within wheels, Maggiotto thought, fascinated by her shrewdness. "It's weird," he pointed out, "that no matter what Cecelia says, the two of you are able to talk about it. But at the same time you claim that you never had any detailed conversations about it."

"Exactly!" Pam responded, slipping away yet again. "You'll notice that Cecelia is the one talking about all the details and I'm the one agreeing."

Another reason she continued to refuse to go to the authorities, she added, was that she wanted to talk to Bill first, to confront him with what Cecelia had told her and see if he would admit to the murder. She was still having trouble believing Cecelia on that point, Pam claimed. Bill just did not seem like a murderer.

She was trying to devise a way of contacting him without being obvious, she contended, when she hit upon the idea of anonymously sending to his mother the audio tape he had given her the day after they made love for the first time. Pam said she knew Mrs. Flynn would give the tape to Bill and he would know it was from Pam and then *he* would make the move to contact her. Except he did not. She still was trying to work out a solution to that problem when she was arrested.

"I used very poor judgment and I'm sorry for that," she said, sounding totally uncontrite. "But I had nothing to do with the murder of my husband."

"Honesty is the best policy in your book, right?" asked Maggiotto, not moved by her apparent display of candor.

"Apparently not always," she replied, indicating they understood each other very well.

Rather than *telling* the police, she continued, she wanted them to be confused. That way she could buy time to complete her own investigation. Perhaps, she admitted, if Bill himself had confessed to her, she might then have gone to the authorities. But only then.

"If it came down to keeping the affair secret or giving the police information, the affair always won out?" he asked.

"Yes."

"But you have to admit that you were withholding information," he persisted. "It's on tape."

For the first time she hinted that she might be tiring of the cat-and-mouse game. "If I was guilty," she said, "I would have pleaded guilty and plea-bargained with the rest of them."

Angrily Maggiotto asked the judge to strike that response from the record and order the jury to disregard it. Gray agreed, but the words were already out. They had been heard, and erasing them from memory was not as easy as the judge's order.

When Pam was interviewed by investigators on June 20, the prosecutor pointed out, reading from a police transcript, she had told them that she had urged Cecelia to tell them everything she knew.

"That was a bald-faced lie," he said accusingly, referring to the tapes in which Pam contradicted what she had told the officers.

"That's right," she replied, unabashed.

"Were you trying to impress the police with your honesty?" Maggiotto asked. "Wasn't that the same day you said, 'I'm going to tell you the honest-to-God truth?' It seems that your honest-to-God truth' switches as you go along."

"Right," Pam agreed. "At that time it did." But so what? she continued, confessing that she had made a mistake.

"You have made a lot of mistakes so far in this case, haven't you?"

"Yeah, I sure have."

"Was killing your husband one of those mistakes?"

"No, it wasn't."

"Was not getting a divorce one of them?"

"No," she repeated stubbornly. "I didn't want to get a divorce."

As they went along, Pam's testimony got increasingly complicated.

By the time Cecelia strolled into her office on

July 12 for still another tape-recorded conversation, Pam related, she was overtly trying to talk her friend out of going to the police. The reason, she said, was that she wanted to get more information from her before *she* was ready to go to the authorities.

"I wanted to know if Bill was involved," she asserted. "I didn't want to accuse someone of murder until I was sure in my own mind that he was."

If her reason for not reporting what she knew to investigators was that she was conducting her own investigation, Maggiotto asked, how come she was not asking Cecelia direct questions rather than simply going with the flow of the conversation?

"I don't need to ask questions to get information," Pam replied. "Every time I was around Cecelia she talked about the murder and information just came out."

For example, she said, Cecelia told her that the murderers had dropped a glove when they ran from the condo. "And I said, 'Oh, yeah, they dropped a glove.' But that was the first I had heard about it. I'm supposed to have known about this beforehand so I'm not going to ask her two hundred questions."

No, Maggiotto disagreed. What she was trying to do was scare Cecelia out of going to the police.

"Exactly," she agreed.

"You're scaring her. You're telling her that if

she goes to the authorities, she's going to be charged as an accessory to murder."

"Exactly."

"Why didn't *you* tell the police?" he asked yet again.

"Because I wasn't thinking rationally."

When she said that "nothing was going wrong until they fucking told Ralph," she meant that nothing was going wrong for *them,* not for her, she contended. If she had implied that she knew about the plan, that was just a continuation of her earlier statement that she knew about the murder beforehand, because obviously if she had known about the murder, then naturally she would have known about the plan. Pam waved a copy of the transcript of the July 12 conversation with Cecelia. "This whole entire thing is a fabrication," she said.

"Yeah," Maggiotto agreed. "On *your* part."

"On Cecelia's part, too," Pam shot back, "because *she* knew she was being recorded."

The entire purpose of the July 12 conversation, Pam admitted, was to try to talk Cecelia out of going to the police and to get information.

"That doesn't make sense," Maggiotto said.

"It doesn't make much sense now, but when someone you love is murdered, you do things you might not do otherwise," Pam said.

Doggedly the prosecutor continued to press her for details about the July 12 meeting with Cecelia.

"To tell you the truth," Pam interrupted, "I don't even remember the entire day. I was under stress. I was on medication. My mind was racing. I was confused. I was scared. I had heard rumors. I was in a state of hysteria and desperation. And the voice on the tape lends to that."

Why had she simply not told the truth? Maggiotto persisted. How could the jury be expected to believe her, he asked, when she had failed to be honest with the police, with Gregg's parents, with her parents, with her friends, and with Cecelia?

"I wasn't in a court of law then."

"Oh," he responded in frustration. "That makes a difference?"

"It sure does," Pam said smoothly.

Maggiotto shrugged. "No further questions," he said, taking his seat.

Without a trace of emotion on her face, Pam stepped down from the witness box and glided to her seat. She had been under cross-examination for much of two days, and she had never wavered in her story. She was, Maggiotto had to agree, one shrewd witness.

30

Pam's testimony was the climax of the trial. After she left the stand, public interest declined considerably, but the proceeding was not yet over. Twomey and Sisti still had a handful of witnesses they wanted to call to tie up some loose ends, and both sides still had their summations to present.

Patricia McGuiness, a tall, blond bank officer wearing a purple dress, was summoned by Sisti to testify that there had been no transactions in Pam's checking account to substantiate Bill's testimony that Pam had withdrawn a small amount of cash on May 1 or a few days before, money that allegedly was used to buy the bullets that killed Gregg. On cross-examination, however, Maggiotto confirmed that if Pam had used a credit card rather than a bank card at her ATM, the record would not be reflected in her bank statements. Neither would it show up if she'd cashed a check written by someone else.

As far as McGuiness went, her testimony was

a standoff: the defense showed the money Bill said he received from Pam apparently did not come from Pam's account, but that did not rule out the possibility that it had come from another source.

A more positive witness for the defense was Patty Weisser, Pam's former secretary at SAU 21. Weisser corroborated Pam's claims that on May 1 Pam had been with a group from the office that attended a luncheon in Portsmouth and did not get back to Hampton until after classes had ended for the day at Winnacunnet High. This testimony was designed to counter Cecelia's assertion that Pam had told her that afternoon that the murder was going to take place in a few hours.

The prosecution could offer no significant counterclaim to show that Cecelia had indeed met with Pam that day as she contended, but Nicolosi was able to draw a concession from Weisser that it was *possible* Pam and Cecelia had crossed paths at some point during the day outside of a formal meeting in Pam's office.

One of the defense's final witnesses was a stocky young man named Brian Washburn, who claimed to have been Gregg's best friend. A self-employed screen printer with blond hair that tumbled six inches or more below his shoulders, Washburn was called to give added weight to Pam's claims that she did indeed have a plan to elicit information about Gregg's murder from

Cecelia, thereby weakening the prosecution's position that Pam and Cecelia had merely been exchanging confidences during their recorded conversations.

Washburn, however, turned out to be a disaster. Before he left the stand, he did considerably more damage to the defense, whose case he was there to bolster, than he did to the prosecution.

Under questioning by Twomey, Washburn confirmed that he had known Gregg since 1983 and that he had considered the dead man his best friend. They used to go everywhere together, he said, including periodic weekend jaunts to Atlantic City, where Gregg was particularly fond of the card game baccarat.

On their last trip to the casinos in mid-April, some two weeks before he was killed, Washburn said Gregg seemed edgy and was drinking more than normal. Apparently looking for a friendly ear, Gregg had confided in his friend.

"Everything is all screwed up," Washburn quoted Gregg as saying. Then he elaborated upon the remark by adding: "Don't tell anybody this, but I screwed this other girl, and any time Pam and I get in a fight she always brings it up."

Washburn said he commiserated with his friend but implied that he felt Gregg had created much of his own problem by admitting his infidelity to Pam.

The last time he had seen Gregg was the Sunday before his murder, but he had talked to him briefly the day he was murdered. Gregg had called him, suggesting they get together for lunch, but Washburn had not been able to make it.

That night he received a call from his girlfriend, Tracy Collins, who said Pam had called her and told her that Gregg had been murdered. He immediately went to Judith and William Smart's house and found Pam either sitting or kneeling on the floor. "She just kept asking, 'Why would anyone want to do this?'"

In the weeks following the murder, he said, he and his girlfriend got closer to Pam, and she began confiding in them her plans to elicit information from Cecelia.

"I remember one time when I was at her house and she had talked about ways of finding out what had happened—" Washburn began before Nicolosi cut him off with an objection.

The defense attempt to inject that testimony lost considerable steam when Washburn admitted he was not sure of the date the conversation took place, although he was almost certain it was before the last of Pam's recorded conversations with Cecelia.

Trying to recoup, Twomey asked Washburn if Pam had mentioned how she planned to get the information from Cecelia.

"She said, 'I wonder if I act like I know something about this, if she'll say something to me.'"

"Did you respond?" asked Twomey.

"Yeah," Washburn agreed. "I told her not to be an a-hole."

On cross-examination, however, Nicolosi quickly undid any good the defense might have achieved in calling Washburn.

With a series of concise questions, Nicolosi established that Washburn had mentioned only half of his Atlantic City conversation with Gregg. In addition to confiding that Pam brought up his infidelity every time they got in an argument, Gregg also told Washburn that "she would not be able to do that anymore." Asked what he meant by that, Washburn said that Gregg told him that Pam also had an affair, so she would no longer be able to accuse him of something she also had done.

The significance of this admission was that Pam had testified that she had not told Gregg about her affair with Bill until just a few days before he was killed, but if Washburn's testimony was accurate, Gregg knew about it at least a few *weeks* before May 1.

Although that discovery was important, Nicolosi was just getting warmed up. In addition to his incomplete testimony before the court, she contended that Washburn also had been less than forthright with investigators.

Reading from a police report, Nicolosi pointed out that two days after Gregg's murder he had told police that "everything was going fine" in Gregg's life and he knew of no reason why anyone would have wanted him dead.

"Did you tell them about Gregg Smart having an extramarital affair?" Nicolosi asked.

"No," Washburn admitted.

"Did you tell them that Gregg told you he knew that Pam had had an extramarital affair?"

"No."

"In fact," Nicolosi persisted, "you didn't even tell the jury that just now?"

He admitted he had not.

Why had he not told anyone about such a significant bit of information? the prosecutor wanted to know.

Washburn shrugged. "I promised Gregg I wouldn't tell," he responded lamely.

Nicolosi, however, did not want to let it drop. "You never thought that maybe a scorned lover of the defendant might have been Gregg's killer?" she asked in feigned amazement.

Washburn tried to evade the issue by saying that he had no details of the alleged trysts. But Nicolosi wanted to make sure the jury understood the relevance of her line of questioning.

"It's possible that a scorned lover of Pamela Smart could have killed him, isn't it?" she asked.

"Yes," Washburn admitted.

"And it's possible that a scorned lover of Gregg Smart could have killed him?"

"Yes."

"And you didn't tell the police that?" she asked haughtily.

"Nope."

Still Nicolosi was not through. When, she demanded, had Washburn finally shared his information with the police?

Washburn admitted it was only after the trial started and only after he had first gone to the defense attorneys, volunteering to be a witness for Pam.

Speaking of Pam, Nicolosi said, it appeared that Washburn and his girlfriend had become even friendlier with her after Gregg's murder. In the first month she was behind bars, Nicolosi pointed out, Washburn and his girlfriend had visited Pam four times.

Before letting Washburn go, Nicolosi had one more fact she wanted to establish.

"Do you have a lawyer?" she asked abruptly.

Washburn admitted that he did.

"Why?" Nicolosi asked.

"Because people keep sending me checks," he responded, adding that the money was coming from producers interested in a possible movie about the Gregg Smart case.

"What is the size of these checks?" Nicolosi asked coldly.

"I received one for two thousand dollars," he said.

Nicolosi nodded. "It's okay," she said, "to enter into a contract and make money off the death of your best friend, right?"

Washburn looked down and took a long time to answer. "Everybody else is," he mumbled.

Nicolosi said nothing. Then, after another pause, Washburn added: "No, it's not all right."

31

PAUL TWOMEY, THE FORMER special-education teacher who was driven to the law because of his empathy for emotionally disturbed youths who found themselves in trouble with the authorities, had nothing but contempt for the teenagers who pointed their fingers at his client, Pam Smart.

Draping his long frame over the podium, which had been turned to face the jury box rather than the witness stand, Twomey began a blistering summation in which he attacked Bill, J.R., and Pete as "vermin" and "weasels" who conspired to lie about Pam when it appeared that they were going to be called to account for the "thrill killing" of Gregory Smart.

"They're vicious animals," he said, speaking as softly as he had when he questioned Pam during direct examination. "They're not human beings worthy of belief. They're bad people." Plus, they had made a pact with the devil. "Those three don't have to worry about spending the rest of their lives in prison," he claimed, pointing out that they received their reward in the form of reduced sentences.

In an attempt to create doubt in the minds of the jurors, Twomey laid out a list of still unsolved mysteries about Gregg's murder, mysteries that were not addressed at any depth during the testimony phase of the trial.

First, there was the mystery of the brass candlestick that had been found on the floor near Gregg's body. Bill had testified that he hefted the candlestick while waiting for Gregg to come home and had briefly considered using it as a club to bring Gregg under his and Pete's control. In the end, though, he said he rejected the idea and simply put the candlestick down. No testimony was presented to explain how it got near the victim's body or why it was there.

Then, said Twomey, there was the mystery of the towel, the one that Pete had claimed he and Bill initially considered using to throw over Gregg's head and drag him inside when he opened the door. Pete asserted that they rejected that idea as well and simply threw it on the floor. It was never determined how or why it ended up near the body.

There also was a puzzle—or at least the defense wanted to create one—concerning the gunshot wound to Gregg's head. Twomey said testimony from one of Pam and Gregg's neighbors indicated the shot that killed Gregg had been muffled, a contention consistent with testimony from the pathologist, who said there may have been an "intermediate target" between the gun and Gregg's head. That is, the killer or killers used something to try to quiet the sound of a gunshot. But none of the youths mentioned using any such device.

But the biggest mystery of all, Twomey said, was the one surrounding Gregg's ring. Although both Pete and Bill denied removing or forcing Gregg to remove his ring, it was found on the floor near the body. According to the pathologist, there were injuries on Gregg's finger consistent with those that would have been suffered if a ring had been "forcibly removed." How, when, why, and by whom this was done was never explained.

Twomey did not offer solutions to any of these questions; he only raised them to show that the picture of what happened inside unit 4E on the night of May 1 was still incomplete. The fact that there were so many holes in the prosecution's case was sufficient cause for the jury to reject the state's position, he argued.

"Something unspeakable happened in that house," Twomey declared ominously. "They did something else. They tortured that man in some way they won't talk about."

Still smarting from the muddle that resulted from Brian Washburn's testimony, Twomey accused the prosecutors of "treating him worse than they treated the three murderers," whom the defense attorney attacked individually.

"You can feel sorry for Billy Flynn if you want,

but [empathy] doesn't have anything to do with this case," Twomey contended. The image the jury had received of Bill was that he was like a "little puppy dog," while he was, in fact, a cold-blooded killer searching for thrills and power. "Is he the little boy who cried here, or is he the heartless punk who laughed on his way to jail?"

Pete, the defense attorney argued, was an emotionless robot whose dream was to be a professional assassin. "He has the emotions of a slug," Twomey said, then immediately corrected himself. "No, he doesn't," he added. "He has the emotions of a rock. If you stick a pin in a slug, it moves. It feels pain. But Pete Randall doesn't know human emotions."

Bill and Pete were on opposite ends of the emotional spectrum, Twomey said, spreading his arms to demonstrate the distance between them. "Emotions—thrill-killing forces—course right through Billy's body. He cries at the drop of a hat. He is obsessed with the love of Pamela Smart and the hatred of Gregory Smart."

He polished off J.R. in a few curt sentences, dubbing him "Lattime the liar"—a phrase he sounded out slowly in his pronounced New England accent, "Lat-uh-meh the lie-uh"—before switching his attention to Cecelia.

"What motivates her?" he asked rhetorically. "I don't think we have a clue." She made false reports to investigators, he pointed out, and admitted under oath that she lied to police. Shaking his head as if embarrassed by the state's failure to file charges against her, he reminded the jury that her actions were "crimes in the state of New Hampshire." He urged jurors to listen carefully when Judge Gray defined the crime of conspiracy for them and to ask themselves if Cecelia's actions also did not fit that description of the crime.

"Cecelia is guilty of conspiracy to commit first-degree murder," he declared, "and also aiding and abetting. She attempted to get a gun to kill someone," he said, his voice rising in outrage, "but they give her a 'walk out.'"

As for Pam, his client, he urged jurors to listen to the tapes and note how her voice reflected how she was becoming increasingly frantic in her attempts to find out who had killed her husband. The tapes indeed were "damning," he conceded, but all they really proved was that she had poor judgment, that she was a "basket case" who was trying desperately to find her husband's killer. "I want you to listen to those tapes. She is clearly guilty of having an affair with a minor and of witness tampering, but that doesn't make her guilty of murder."

What it boiled down to, Twomey said, was that he and Sisti had not demonstrated that Pam was innocent. At the same time, that was not their job; the burden of proof was not on the defense, but on the prosecution. What he wanted the jury to remember was that the state was required to show that she was guilty. "I won't tell you we've proven beyond a reasonable doubt that

Pam is innocent, but there are multiple reasons she's not guilty."

Pausing, he ran his gaze over each juror, striving for eye contact. Softly he added: "Do the right thing."

Paul Maggiotto, who handled the summation for the prosecution, was just as indignant as Twomey, except he viewed the situation from a different perspective.

Turning slightly to face Pam, Maggiotto asked the jury to recall the thrust of her argument. What she was claiming, he said, was that a whole string of prosecution witnesses had come forward as part of a widespread conspiracy designed to, in the defense's words, "mastermind the most vile concoction ever to come into a New Hampshire courtroom." Why would they be lying? he asked. After a dramatic pause, he spit out the words: *"To get her?"* He shrugged, using body language to finish the thought, which clearly was, How ridiculous can you get?

"You don't have to waste a moment of deliberation on who killed Gregg Smart," he continued. All the jury had to do was listen to the tapes, and everything they had heard during the two weeks of testimony would click into place.

"You listen to the tapes and you'll see what she was doing," he argued. "As the circle was closing in, Pamela Smart was doing everything in her power to set up a defense; to keep Cecelia quiet; to keep the police off the track."

Conceding one point to the defense, Maggiotto acknowledged that his star witnesses were not going to win any awards for ethics. "No question about it," he agreed, "they are despicable individuals. We didn't put them on the stand for you to like them. We put them on the stand for you to evaluate if they are telling the truth." The jury may not have *liked* what they had to say; they had only to *believe* it. "I submit to you," he said, "that if Bill Flynn was lying, that is one of the greatest performances you've seen in modern times." Granted, he said, Bill was a punk with a history of petty crime. But even that may have been part of Pam's grand plan. "She didn't approach the class valedictorian to commit this crime."

To understand the dimensions of the scheme that resulted in Gregg's murder, the prosecutor suggested, the jury had to focus closely on the real motive and ignore the smoke screen that Pam had tried to create. "We're not suggesting she killed Gregg Smart for the insurance money. We're not suggesting she killed for the furniture." At its core, her reason was more ethereal. "She was very, very concerned with her image," Maggiotto proposed. "If they got a divorce, the affair would have come out. It was going to ruin her reputation. She was going to lose her job." And, he added, she undoubtedly would have trouble finding another one. The only solution open to her at that point was murder. And her tool for accomplishing it was Bill Flynn.

Believing in his own heart that Pam's fondness for Bill was genuine, the prosecutor nevertheless was equally convinced that she had manipulated him, with sex, into murdering her husband. By the time she started planning the murder, Maggiotto said, "her hook was so deep into the kid's psyche, so deep into his hormones, he would be willing to participate."

Maggiotto scoffed at the defense idea that the youths referred to by Twomey as "the gang" (Bill, Pete, J.R., and Cecelia), had made up their testimony simply because they saw Pam as a potential scapegoat when they found themselves in serious trouble. If they made up the whole thing, Maggiotto asked the jury, why didn't they do a better job? They had plenty of time and opportunity to work on the fabrication, but in the end there were enough inconsistencies to make people wonder. The fact that those inconsistencies were there gave their tale a large amount of credibility, he said.

Returning to the main players, Maggiotto ticked them off yet again for the jury's benefit.

Take Pete, for example. "There's no doubt," he admitted, "that Pete is a cold, calculating murderer. This crime could not have happened without Pete."

But balance that, he urged, with the testimony of Ralph Welch, who was *not* one of the members of the group, but whose testimony substantiated that given by Bill, Pete, J.R., and Cecelia. Ralph heard Pete and J.R. talking about the murder, and when cornered, Pete admitted their role as well as volunteering statements about Pam's involvement. That was *before* they were arrested, Maggiotto pointed out. At that stage, Bill, Pete, and J.R. had no reason to bring in Pam because they did not need a scapegoat. "They didn't know Ralph Welch was going to go to the police. He was a trusted friend."

As for Cecelia, he reminded the jurors that there was not a single piece of testimony to show that Cecelia was "in cahoots" with the others.

Additionally, Maggiotto said, there were two witnesses who spent only minutes on the stand when they were called, but whose testimony was exceedingly important, not because it related to firsthand knowledge of Pam's involvement, but because it corroborated what the major witnesses had said about Pam.

One of them, the prosecutor recalled, was Cindy Butt, a woman who had worked with Cecelia at Papa Gino's. Her testimony had been brief, but it was nevertheless very important because she had told how Cecelia had mentioned a month before Gregg was killed that she had a friend named Pam who wanted her husband murdered. "There was no motive for Cecelia to lie at that time."

Another of the witnesses whose testimony the jury should recall, Maggiotto said, was George Moses, whose mother was on the same cell block as Pam in the women's prison. George said Pam had wanted him to testify that he had heard

Cecelia plotting Pam's frame-up. But, Maggiotto added, George had gone to investigators early in November and told them about the approach. That, the prosecutor pointed out, was three months before J.R., Bill, and Pete had confessed.

"That's the beauty of the state's case," he explained: the prosecution had so many witnesses.

In addition to the corroborating testimony, Maggiotto said, there was, "above all," the words of Pam herself. "She can't deny those tapes exist," he said. "She can't deny she didn't make the statements." Mocking the idea that anything else was needed to prove Pam's guilt, Maggiotto concluded: "The only thing you're missing is a videotape of her conversations with Bill Flynn."

Twomey had talked for almost an hour and Maggiotto for a little more than an hour. But the jury was not quite ready to begin deliberations. Before they were locked into a room to decide Pam's fate, there was one more person to hear from: Judge Gray. Up to that point, the jurors had heard hours upon hours of raw testimony, certainly enough for them to be forming their own ideas about Pam's guilt or innocence. But they still needed the judge to put the issues into a legal perspective. It was not simply a matter of whether Pam had done it or not, but a question of how their opinions fit into the confines of the law. Their decisions would have to be couched in legal terms, and it was Gray's duty to explain to them what those legal parameters were.

32

FORMALLY, PAM WAS ACCUSED of three fel-
onies: conspiracy to commit murder, being an
accomplice to first-degree murder, and witness
tampering.

By far the most serious was accomplice to
murder, which, upon conviction, carried a mandatory sentence of life in prison without parole.
For jurors to find her guilty on that count, they
first had to make a subtle distinction about
degrees of murder. Pam was accused of being an
accomplice to *first-degree* murder. Although
Gregg undoubtedly was dead and just as
unquestionably had been murdered, Bill had
pleaded guilty to *second-degree* murder, so the
fact that Pam's husband had been murdered in
the first degree was not a given.

To determine first-degree murder, the jury
first had to agree that Gregg had been killed
with "purpose, premeditation, and deliberation." Only if the group decided that first-degree
murder applied could they begin deliberating on

whether Pam, beyond a reasonable doubt, had helped plan or commit the crime. If they agreed unanimously that she had, the verdict would be guilty.

To help them along in their discussions on that count, Gray reminded the jurors that according to the prosecution, Pam had suggested to Bill that he wear dark clothes and gloves, and that he ransack the condo so it would appear that a burglary had taken place. Additionally she allegedly had left a door open and made arrangements to be away from the condo on the evening the murder occurred—all accusations that, if found to have substance, might help the jury determine if she had taken part in planning the crime.

For jurors to convict her of conspiracy to commit murder, they would have to agree unanimously that Pam acted "purposely" and in concert with one or more others "to commit or cause the commission" of murder. Furthermore, one or more of the co-conspirators would actually have to make an "overt act" in that direction. An overt act could include helping to procure a gun or even something a lot less threatening, such as drawing a map, which is what Bill claimed Pam did for him when he bungled the April attempt to kill Gregg, saying he got lost en route to the condo. Significantly, an actual murder does not have to be committed.

The least serious of the three charges was that

of witness tampering. To convict Pam on that count, the jury would have to agree that Pam had attempted to coerce Cecelia either not to testify or to testify falsely.

Before turning the issues over to the jury, Gray imparted one more observation: Remember, he said, that the audiotapes of Pam and Cecelia's conversations were the official version of what had transpired rather than the transcripts of the recordings. To be absolutely accurate in their deliberations, jurors should rely on the recordings instead of the written record.

It was interesting that Judge Gray also underlined the importance of the tapes. Both the prosecution and the defense had urged the jurors to listen to the recordings as well. The import of that was that lawyers from both sides had stressed the relevance of the tapes for totally dissimilar reasons. The defense hoped the jurors would listen to them and decide that Pam was a passive participant and was trying only to elicit information from Cecelia. The prosecution, on the other hand, hoped the jury would listen to them and come to the opposite conclusion.

The jury, not surprisingly, would place a lot of emphasis on the tapes. And in the end, only the prosecution would be happy with the results.

Pam Smart's case went to the jury late in the day on Wednesday, March 20. It took the group of seven women and five men three days—actually only thirteen hours of deliberation—to reach its verdict of guilty on all three counts, a story that was told very succinctly in a headline in the March 23 edition of the *Union Leader*. There were three lines of large type with one word on each line: GUILTY! GUILTY! GUILTY!

When the verdict was read, Pam, wearing a lavender and plaid black coat and a black skirt, remained as stony as she had throughout the trial. Not even when Judge Gray read the sentence on the accomplice charge, as required by law—imprisonment for the remainder of her life without the possibility of parole—did she flinch.

Sisti, in fact, seemed more shocked than his client. "I thought we established reasonable doubt," he groaned, adding that there likely would be an appeal.

Maggiotto and Nicolosi accepted the verdicts quietly, without celebration. "I think justice was done," Maggiotto told reporters. "There was no question in our minds the evidence was there."

The Smarts, who had sat solemnly throughout the trial, frequently fighting back tears when testimony got too graphic, cheered when the verdicts were read. "Thank God," mumbled Gregg's father, William. "Thank Paul Maggiotto."

Pam's parents, John and Linda Wojas, declined comment.

What was surprising to most of those who had sat through the trial or followed it closely via the media was not so much the decision, but how harmoniously it was reached. According to one of the jurors, a young graduate student named Alec Beckett, there was never any serious dissension among the group concerning Pam's guilt.

A week after the verdicts, Beckett wrote a story about the deliberations for the Boston *Globe*. In it he gave a rare and remarkable peek at what went on behind closed doors when twelve strangers were thrown together and asked to make a decision of such magnitude.

According to Beckett, jurors, who had been cautioned not to discuss the case either among themselves or with others for the duration of the trial, initially felt some unease at being freed to argue the points they had heard discussed for more than two weeks. The ice was broken, however, when one woman nervously took the floor late that first afternoon and remarked on how she thought it was strange that Pam would have taken off work on May 1, a day when she had hardly been in the office at all anyway, to drive Bill, whom she had supposedly broken up with several days before, to Haverhill just because he asked.

To prove that they had been attentive when Twomey had made his summation, the jury spent a sizable amount of time discussing the "mysteries" that he had brought up, specifically the candlestick that was found near Gregg's body. They also debated whether Pam had ever truly loved Bill; whether her reasons for attending the school board meeting on the night

her husband was murdered were real or manu-
factured; and how much knowledge Bill had
about Gregg's life insurance policies. This latter
was vital to the defense argument because
Twomey had insisted there was no way Pam or
anyone else could have known the value of the
policy which he had through his employer—the
one that eventually totaled $90,000—until it
was calculated after his death.

In all, Beckett wrote, the two and a half hours
they spent discussing the case on Wednesday
was basically an exploratory period they used to
kick ideas back and forth. At the end of that day
three jurors were firmly convinced of Pam's
guilt and three said they still had some reserva-
tions. The other six were fairly noncommittal,
but no one spoke up for a verdict of not guilty.

On the second day, Thursday, March 21, they
began to get down to business. Being practical
people, they tackled the easiest charge first.
Since Twomey had virtually admitted during
his summation that Pam had tried to pressure
Cecelia, the group voted quickly, without dissension, that she was guilty on the charge of witness
tampering. The other two charges, however,
prompted considerable debate. But the one
thing they agreed upon was that they needed to
listen carefully to the tapes.

As they played the recordings, Pam's little-girl
voice belied her words: ""I'm, like, what the
fucking hell is going on. . . . You'd have to be
fucking deranged to say okay. . . . I can't even

fucking believe this. . . . They're fucking wicked expensive. . . . Nothing was going wrong until they fucking told Ralph. . . . They're going to fucking bludgeon you to death . . . if you send me to the fucking slammer . . ."

After listening to what seemed like an interminable string of the same Anglo-Saxon verb, one of the jurors could not restrain himself. "I think," Beckett quoted him as saying, "we have no choice but to find her fucking guilty."

The humor was short-lived; immediately they were back to debating the issues . . . and listening to tapes. The more they listened, the more convinced they became that the tapes spoke more convincingly about the circumstances surrounding Gregg's murder than did Pam's testimony.

"Slowly," Beckett wrote, "the doubts that several jurors had as a result of the inconsistencies and alternatives that the defense had pointed out in the tapes were simply overwhelmed by the sound of the defendant subtly, and not so subtly, incriminating herself."

By late in the afternoon on the second day, the group was agreed that the prosecution had proved her guilt. However, a formal vote was delayed until the next day because three members wanted to ponder the matter overnight.

The next morning, although the feeling was that unanimity had been reached, they procrastinated on a vote. When a ballot was called after lunch, it was on the conspiracy charge. The vote was 12–0. The same was true on the accomplice charge: the vote was 12–0 on the first ballot.

Other jurors who talked to reporters afterward agreed that the tapes had done Pam in—that and her steely facade.

Charlotte Jefts, seventy-five, told the *Union Leader* that no matter which way the group examined the evidence, they always arrived at the same conclusion: There was never a serious question about Pam's guilt. "We picked every word apart to see if there was a shadow of a doubt, to see if she was not guilty, and we could not find anything. There was just too much evidence against her."

Pam's demeanor also worked against her, the juror added. Her apparent inability to show emotion made Jefts think of a schizophrenic.

Norma Honor, a forty-six-year-old nurse who served as forewoman, told the *Globe* that the evidence, especially the tapes, was too overwhelming. "I didn't want it to turn out this way, but the evidence . . . proved in our minds that she was guilty."

After the verdicts were announced in court and jurors were polled to make sure that they had all been in agreement, Judge Gray met briefly with the group behind closed doors. Volunteering that juries always were curious about how he himself would have voted in a particular case, Gray told them they were going to be disappointed: he was not going to tell them.

But just before he released them, the mood in the room lightened and one of the jurors jokingly asked Gray which actor he hoped would represent him in the movie of the Pam Smart case. Much to his later regret, Gray responded.

"Clint Eastwood," he quipped.

His unguarded remark was not the only thing that would come back to haunt him about the trial, however. Although there had been remarkably little dissension inside the jury room, there was a considerable fury brewing outside. And much of it revolved around Judge Gray's decision not to sequester the jury until the second night of deliberations.

33

As STRANGE AS IT MAY SEEM in states where juries are sequestered as a matter of course, Judge Gray was operating under historical precedent in New Hampshire. Before Pam's trial, a jury had not been locked away during deliberations in a criminal case anywhere in the state for almost seven years.

No one seems exactly sure how or why the practice of nonsequestration was adopted, but most court watchers figure it was for one of two reasons. One school believes New Hampshirites are inherently stingy and judges are reluctant to sequester jurors because they don't want to spend the money for their food and lodging. The other school is convinced that judges hesitate because they sense that jurors themselves don't like it, and as elected officials they do not want to make voters angry. Whatever the reasons, a New Hampshire jury was last sequestered in 1984 when a group was deliberating first-degree murder charges against a former marine named

Gary Place. His trial drew quite a bit of publicity because he claimed that he was suffering from posttraumatic stress disorder as a result of his experiences in Vietnam and that had led him to kill his fiancée. Place subsequently was convicted.

At Pam's trial, a third reason for not sequestering the jury was proffered. It was suggested that jurors were not locked away the first night because no one had told them in advance to bring a suitcase with a change of clothes and toiletries.

In any case, the failure to sequester the jury from the very beginning caused all sorts of problems, primarily because it was on the top of the defense list as a reason for seeking a new trial.

Complicating the issue was a claim by Pam's mother, Linda Wojas, that she received a telephone call on the first night of deliberations from an unidentified man who said he had heard one of the jurors discussing the case publicly—a strict no-no in trial procedures.

The call itself was documentable because law enforcement authorities had put a semipermanent tap on the Wojases' telephone to help protect them from crank calls. When the man telephoned, his message was taped.

Pam's mother said as soon as she heard about the incident she asked for a meeting with Judge Gray and was ushered into his office on Thursday, the second day of deliberations. She said Gray summoned the juror who allegedly was talking about the case and questioned the juror regarding the accusation. According to Mrs. Wojas, Gray was satisfied that the prohibition against discussing the case had not been violated, and he allowed the deliberations to continue. On March 28, six days after the jury returned its verdicts, the state attorney general's office said it had investigated the report and had determined that no improper action occurred.

But even without that incident, Sisti and Twomey figured they had ample basis for requesting a new trial. Other factors they hinted they might raise included Judge Gray's refusal before the trial started to grant a defense request for change of venue based on excessive publicity surrounding the case; the legality of allowing Cecelia to be wired considering she was a minor; and a claim that the prosecution did not give the defense all the information it was entitled to regarding details of the pact police made with Cecelia when she agreed to wear the body wire. Another possible issue, the lawyers said, might be Judge Gray's refusal to permit defense attorneys to recall Bill after he had testified for the prosecution. According to Twomey, the defense received information indicating that Bill had been acting when he'd tearfully recounted Gregg's murder. Some observers said Gray's refusal to bring him back as a defense witness might have violated Pam's constitutional right to question her accuser.

No matter which way Gray turned, he seemed

to be in trouble. As for his unfortunate comment about Clint Eastwood representing him in a possible movie about the Smart case, the judge told the Boston *Globe* that the remark had been entered in jest in an attempt to relieve posttrial tension among jurors.

"It was made simply to relax them and give them a bit of humor," Gray told the newspaper.

The judge's attempt at humor was one of the few efforts at levity by any of the major participants. Mainly, the comments after the trial were as acrimonious as the testimony that had been presented during the proceeding.

The Smarts, of course, were delighted with the outcome.

Judith Smart, Gregg's mother, said the tension was unbearable when the jury came back into the room after deliberations. "I lost my breath," she said. "It seemed an eternity before the word *guilty* came out of [the jury forewoman's] mouth." But once it did, she "wanted to scream and holler."

A jubilant William Smart proclaimed: "The justice system works in this society. We're very, very happy."

For the most part, though, the other major participants were very *un*happy.

Pam's parents declined to comment after the trial, but her father, John Wojas, told reporters just before the verdicts were read that the trial had been a major humiliation for the family. "We've had tragedies before, but not of this magnitude," he said. "This is something that happens to other people, not to us."

Pam's mother, Linda Wojas, also was quoted as severely criticizing the news coverage of the proceeding, calling it a "circus."

"The only thing missing," she added, "was the cotton candy."

Sisti and Twomey, not surprisingly, were acerbic about the media coverage.

"I think the coverage has been scandalous," groused Sisti.

His partner, Twomey, called it "barely above contemptible," adding, "Do I think the coverage has been biased against my client? Absolutely!"

It was hardly a surprise, but the unhappiest person of all was Pam. And she reacted in a way that area reporters had come to expect. Eight days after she was found guilty, Pam responded to a written request for an interview with the Boston *Globe*.

In the interview, which was conducted by telephone, she lashed out at the prosecutors, the judge, the witnesses who testified against her, the jury, and those she thought stood to make a profit from her predicament. During the interview with the *Globe*'s Bob Hohler, she contended that

- she never thought she would be convicted; the worst she figured could happen was for the trial to end with a hung jury.
- much of the blame for her conviction could be

attributed to the extensive news coverage of the crime and the trial.
- biased news coverage influenced the jury.
- she was so depressed by events that she was seriously contemplating suicide.
- Judge Gray made an unforgivable mistake when he told jurors that he hoped Clint Eastwood would play his character if a movie was made of her saga.
- she felt empathy for Bill when he sobbed on the witness stand, but she put aside that feeling because he was the one who murdered her husband.
- she may have acted strangely after Gregg's murder, but "nobody gave me the twenty-two-year-old widow's handbook."
- her "Ice Princess" image was undeserved; every night in the privacy of her cell she cried herself to sleep.
- the trial received excessive attention because the country was in a recession and the public needed something to get their minds off economic woes.
- her cell is decorated with pictures of Gregg and Halen, her dog.

It was a bitter Pam who spoke with the reporter for the Boston newspaper, one who claimed that she had been put upon, lied about, lied to, and generally mistreated. Ironically, it was cruel refutation of her comment to Cecelia that when it came down to it, a jury would take her word—the word of a professional—over the words of a group of teenagers.

Although Pam claimed before she was arrested that she had been seeing a psychiatrist, there was never any psychiatric evidence presented at her trial, nothing to give the public an expert's view of why she had behaved as she did or what drove her to her eventual end.

If, as many suspected, Pam was motivated by her fear of the loss of her image, her fate is truly hapless. If speculation is accurate that the reason she wanted Gregg murdered was to preserve her reputation and her career, then she has indeed lost almost everything. Her job is gone, as well as her good name, her pride, her family's reputation, and virtually all hope for the future. Verily, to be twenty-three and in prison with no hope of ever being released is perhaps the grimmest of prospects. Bill, Pete, and J.R. face a similar fate, but for them there appears to be at least some sort of resolution. They have hope of being released eventually, although Bill and Pete will be close to middle-aged when that day comes and J.R. will long have lost the bloom of youth.

But in a case that has been filled with ironies, there are two that cannot be overlooked.

Before her world came crashing down, even before the autumn she met Bill, Pam had told friends that her main ambition was to be a TV personality, a star of the airwaves, a figure whose name and face would be recognized by millions. In a perverse way—and certainly not in the manner in which she had dreamed—that ambition has been fulfilled. Her name, her face, and her achievements are indeed familiar to millions. At age twenty-three she became an international figure.

The final irony is that throughout the period beginning with her arrest and continuing through her trial, she has consistently been referred to, albeit erroneously, as a teacher. During her days at Winnacunnet she was the school board's media director, a low-level bureaucrat who never taught a class. But now that she is an inmate, reality has caught up with perception. Her job at the women's state prison is that of teacher. Pam Smart, ex-school district employee, is Pam Smart, inmate instructor of other inmates in high school math, science, and spelling. Her salary: $1.50 a week.

Epilogue

• RAYMOND "RAYME" FOWLER, the fourth
teenager allegedly involved in Gregg's death,
pleaded not guilty to charges of conspiracy to
commit murder and falsifying physical evidence
in connection with the death of Gregg Smart,
and with attempted murder because of an
alleged earlier attempt on Gregg's life. According to authorities, not to mention Bill, Pete, and
J.R., Rayme waited in the car with J.R. the night
Gregg was killed. Furthermore, Bill testified,
Raymond also accompanied him to Derry in an
unsuccessful attempt to murder Gregg in April,
some two weeks before he was actually shot.

According to Raymond's lawyer, Charles Graham of Newburyport, Massachusetts, his client
does not deny being in the car on either trip, but
he *does* deny he was there under the impression
that a murder was planned or would be committed. An admitted petty thief (he had, in fact,
served time in both juvenile and adult facilities
after being convicted of receiving stolen goods),

Raymond claims that he had been told only that, as Graham put it, "property was going to be stolen."

Oddly, Graham added, it was Raymond's statements to police that resulted in the arrests of Bill, Pete, and J.R. Although Ralph Welch had gone to authorities after his conversation with Pete, Graham said, investigators went first to Raymond. When he corroborated what Ralph had told them, investigators sought warrants for the arrests of the other three.

When Raymond is tried in October, a cornerstone of his defense apparently will be that he helped police, much as Cecelia had, in building a case against the murderers. "His complicity was probably not as much and no greater than Cecelia's," Graham contended in a telephone interview. If the attorney general's office had listened to Raymond anytime between June 11 when Pete, J.R. and Bill were arrested and late January when they agreed to a plea-bargain they would, Graham said, "[have] been able to get them all without them having to cut the deal that they did," a pact he called a "deal of a lifetime" for the three.

As for the determination to prosecute Raymond, Graham felt it was mainly a face-saving effort by the attorney general's office to cover its embarrassment for not listening to Raymond before sealing the arrangement with J.R., Bill, and Pete, all of whom undoubtedly will be called to testify against Raymond under the terms of their agreement with the state.

• Although Cecelia admitted on the stand to lying to investigators, to being present when plans for Gregg's murder were discussed, and to two unsuccessful attempts to help Bill locate a gun, no charges have been filed against her and none are contemplated.

• On May 6, Pam was sentenced by Judge Gray for witness tampering and for conspiring to murder her husband. The mandatory sentence of life without parole on the accomplice-to-murder conviction was handed down on March 22 as soon as the jury returned its verdict, but sentencing on the other two convictions was postponed, as is common in such situations. At the May 6 hearing, Judge Gray sentenced Pam to the maximum possible terms on the other two charges: up to fifteen years for conspiracy and up to seven years for witness tampering. Both sentences will run concurrently with the sentence for accomplice to murder.

As is the custom in New Hampshire, the Smarts were allowed at the sentencing hearing to make what is called a victim impact statement, in effect a formal public comment on the case. Speaking for the family, William Smart called Pam a "cold-blooded murderer" and said he hoped it was the last time he ever had to see her face-to-face. In addition, he added, he hoped she lived "a very, very long life."

Wounded by the words, Pam jumped to her feet. "I don't have to take this!" she screamed. "I can't handle this."

Her mother also jumped up and yelled at William Smart, "When is your vengeance going to end?"

On the other side of the courtroom, Judith Smart, Gregg's mother, popped to her feet with her fists clenched.

Apparently fearing a physical confrontation, the bailiff interceded and announced that anyone who wanted to leave the room was free to do so at that time.

Obviously thinking that included her, since she had already announced her desire to leave, Pam stood as if she were going.

Judge Gray stared at her and quickly interjected: "Except the defendant!"

• Pam's lawyers, Sisti and Twomey, had thirty days from the day of sentencing to file an appeal. If it is filed, it probably will be ruled upon, given the state appeals court's promptness, by the end of the year.

• As of May 1991, Bill, Pete, and J.R., were being held in the Rockingham County Jail, but they eventually would be transferred to the main prison in Concord.

• On April 1, 1991, ten days after Pam was found guilty of three charges in connection with her husband's murder and was sentenced to life in prison without possibility of parole, the state attorney general's office dismissed three charges against Pam in Hillsborough County stemming from her alleged attempts to persuade Cecelia not to testify or to have her killed. She had been indicted on January 4 for criminal solicitation of murder, witness tampering, and criminal solicitation involving witness tampering. Although the two principal witnesses against her on these charges, fellow inmates Diana Cullen and Marianne Moses, had been on the prosecution's witness list for Pam's trial, neither was called. The issue became moot when the charges were dismissed.

• There is a strong possibility that Pam's story will make it to the screen. In addition to Cecelia's contract with Once Upon a Time Productions, Brian Washburn, Gregg's self-admitted best friend, has said he is considering several contracts. William and Judith Smart, Gregg's parents, have been approached as well, but they told reporters they would insist upon "creative control" before agreeing to any deal. Pam's parents, John and Linda Wojas, told reporters they were approached as well, but they declined even to consider any such offers.

In addition to a potential movie, it is not too farfetched to imagine that Pam might write a book giving her own version of events. Unlike many states, New Hampshire has no law that would prohibit her from profiting from her own story.

• In a final attempt to remove Pam from their family's memory, William Smart said soon after his former daughter-in-law's conviction that he would change a headstone on Gregg's grave that had been erected by Pam. One side of the pink-gray marble marker was engraved with Gregg's name, along with the dates of his birth and death. The other side carried a large heart, the name *Smart,* and the words *A life that touches the hearts of others, lives on forever.* William Smart said the sentiment was entirely unfitting considering the progression of events, and he would have the stone replaced.

• In addition to possibly seeking a new trial for Pam on the charges for which she was convicted, attorneys Sisti and Twomey said they were considering challenging the law that mandates a sentence of life imprisonment without parole for someone convicted as an accomplice to first-degree murder on grounds that it constitutes cruel and unusual punishment. The state supreme court has upheld the mandatory sentence for someone convicted of murder, but it has not ruled on its appropriateness for an accomplice to murder.

Lisa Steinberg—six years old and defenseless, she was the brutalized victim of a couple's descent into delusion and violence.

Joel Steinberg—cruel and controlling, he ruled his family with intimidation and a deadly iron fist.

Hedda Nussbaum—beaten and brainwashed, did her loyalty to Joel keep her from saving Lisa—or was there a more disturbing reason?

Never before has a trial been so shocking, nor testimony so riveting. Here for the first time is the entire heart-rending story of an outwardly normal family living in the shadow of violence and fear, and the illegally adopted, innocent girl whose life was the price of affection. Retold in the framework of the sensational trial, it is a sad and gripping tale that stabs at the heart's tenderest core.

Documented with 8 pages of gripping photographs

LISA, HEDDA & JOEL

The Steinberg Murder Case

WANTED

True Crime From St. Martin's Paperbacks!

ULTERIOR MOTIVES
by Suzanne Finstad
When Flamboyant tycoon Henry Kyle was found
murdered in 1983, it was only the beginning...
_____ 91185-8 $4.50 U.S. _____ 91186-6 $5.50 Can.

DEADLY BLESSING
by Steve Salerno
The tragic consequences of a marriage between a
wealthy young power broker and a local waitress.
_____ 91215-3 $3.95 U.S. _____ 91216-1 $4.95 Can.

THE SERPENT'S TOOTH
by Christopher P. Anderson
The story of an extremely rich family destroyed by
greed...and murder.
_____ 90541-6 $3.95 U.S. _____ 90542-4 $4.95 Can.

CELLAR OF HORROR
by Ken Englade
What police found in Gary Heidnik's basement went
beyond mere horror...
_____ 90959-4 $4.50 U.S. _____ 90960-8 $5.50 Can.